THE NEW MANAGER'S
SURVIVAL MANUAL

The New Manager's Survival Manual

Second Edition

CLAY CARR

John Wiley & Sons, Inc.

New York • Chichester • Brisbane • Toronto • Singapore

Copyright © 1995 by Clay Carr
Published by John Wiley & Sons, Inc.

Library of Congress Cataloging-in-Publication Data:

Carr, Clay, 1934–
     The new manager's survival manual   /   Clay Carr. — 2nd ed.
       p.   cm.
     Includes index.
     ISBN 0-471-10986-X (cloth). — ISBN 0-471-10987-8 (paper).
     1. Supervision of employees.   2. Employee empowerment.   3. Self-
directed work groups.   I. Title.
HF5549.12.C37   1995
658.3'02—dc20   94-34049

Printed in the United States of America

10 9 8 7 6 5 4 3 2

To Gayle:
Thanks, Honey

Acknowlegements

To my agent, Mike Snell, who suggested this revision, and my editor, John Mahaney, who steered it through the editorial process. My thanks to both of you.

To the staff of the group I try to lead and occasionally to manage—these bright, motivated, and creative people who keep me continually on my toes. I am grateful to each and every one of you.

And to my boss, A.C. Ressler, who could not have been more supportive of us. Thanks.

Preface

WHAT IS THE NEW MANAGER'S SURVIVAL MANUAL?

You're a new manager. Or you're about to become one. Or you want to be one and you want to be prepared when the opportunity comes. *The New Manager's Survival Manual* is written for you. It's the basic guide you need to understand first-level management and to be effective at it.

This book will:

1. Show you what you have to do to be a successful first-level manager.*
2. Show you how to do this, by practicing Phase One Management—what other books often call "supervision."
3. Help you understand the importance of self-managing teams and how they change the management job.
4. Explain Phase Two Management to you, the higher form of management that you want to learn and practice, and also explain why Phase Two Management is essential, even in organizations that use self-managing teams.
5. Start you down the road to successful management—that happy situation where your employees produce, your boss is happy with you, and you are valuable to the organization and promotable.

No single book will tell you everything you need to know or even a tenth of what you need to know. In fact, a dozen books won't tell you all you need.

---

*You may not be familiar with the term *first-level manager*. This is the position that's often called "first-level supervisor," or just "supervisor." As the next chapter will explain, a "supervisor" is first of all a manager—so we're going to call him or her a manager.

This book, though, will get you launched in the right direction, learning the right skills. Because it provides you with practical tips for each aspect of the job, you'll have the basic abilities to deal with anything you may encounter.

Reading this book will also be good preparation for your organization's supervisory and/or managerial development program. After you read it, you'll be able to learn more quickly from the formal training you receive. And because the book doesn't teach one particular way to manage, it will work with whatever managerial style your organization has.

There's another important point, and it's a sort of a pun. *New manager* means someone who has just become a manager—and that's what this book is about. *New manager* also means a manager in the late 1990s, one who performs the job in a way different from the way traditional managers are expected to act. Often, these managers must perform in organizations that are or want to be "empowering" to their workers. This book is especially for these managers, and, if you are one of them, it will prepare you to operate successfully and to contribute value in that environment.

Are you a female manager or would-be manager? If so, this final point is addressed to you. I have consistently used the masculine form. There are other ways to handle the problem of the indeterminate-gender pronoun (he/she, s/he). But because so much of this book is conversation, I believe it would be too confusing to use the slash forms or to alternate male and female pronouns. You will find, however, that there are as many female and male managers, at all levels, who speak through this book—and that, I hope, is the real bottom line.

Contents

Prologue

"Well, how's the division's newest manager today?" Tom smiled at Chuck Weldon as he slipped into the chair across from him.

"He looks a bit bedraggled to me," Jennie said, looking honestly concerned.

"Now, Jennie, didn't your mother ever tell you that if you can't say something nice, etc., etc.?" Eduardo was the fourth person at the table; he was also the oldest and most experienced supervisor by far. "But Chuck does look a little stressed out."

Chuck frowned. "Well, in answer to your question, Tom, I'm feeling very frustrated. Eleanor called in sick again this morning, Bev and Roger aren't speaking to each other and this morning we got four new jobs dumped on us that everybody wants yesterday. Sometimes I don't think I was ever cut out to be in management."

"I know what you mean," Tom said. "I spent the last hour arguing with Reggie about his performance appraisal. I just can't get him to accept that he does just average work. One more hassle like that, and I'm going to give every one of them an 'Above Average' rating and let it go at that—like some people I know have been doing for years." He looked knowingly at Eduardo.

"You're learning. The next thing you need to do is take the personnel policies book and hide it. I have an agreement with my folks—I don't hassle them, they don't hassle me. I haven't had a grievance or an EEO complaint in so long I don't remember what the forms look like."

"Yeah, I know," Jennie agreed gesturing emphatically at Eduardo with her fork. "You let your people get away with murder while the rest of us get a bad name for trying to do what we're supposed to. I was here until eight last night reworking the Emerald Hill project and I'll probably be here just as late tonight redoing something else one of my people screwed up today."

Tom nodded. "You can't get the people they send you these days to do anything on their own. If I didn't stand there and tell them what to do, they wouldn't get a damned thing done. Sometimes I think that I ought to have them call me 'Sarge.'"

Chuck frowned and rested his chin in his hands. "You're sure not helping any! If that's all management is, I'm sorry I took the job. Isn't there some other way to be a first-level manager and still get the job done? . . ."

THE NEW MANAGER'S
SURVIVAL MANUAL

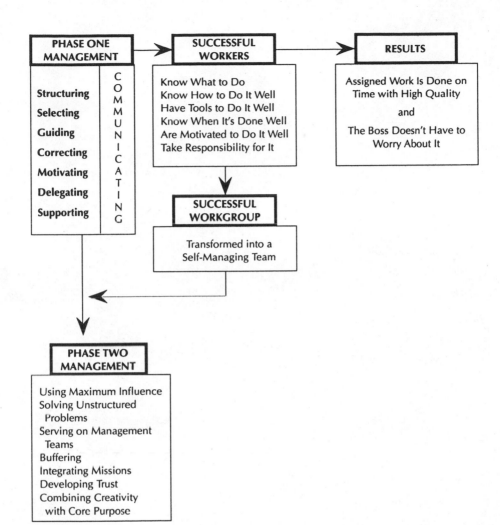

PHASE ONE MANAGEMENT

Structuring
Selecting
Guiding
Correcting
Motivating
Delegating
Supporting

COMMUNICATING

SUCCESSFUL WORKERS

Know What to Do
Know How to Do It Well
Have Tools to Do It Well
Know When It's Done Well
Are Motivated to Do It Well
Take Responsibility for It

RESULTS

Assigned Work Is Done on Time with High Quality

and

The Boss Doesn't Have to Worry About It

SUCCESSFUL WORKGROUP

Transformed into a Self-Managing Team

PHASE TWO MANAGEMENT

Using Maximum Influence
Solving Unstructured
 Problems
Serving on Management
 Teams
Buffering
Integrating Missions
Developing Trust
Combining Creativity
 with Core Purpose

CHAPTER 1

Successful Management: What, How, and the Payoff

A SUCCESSFUL MANAGER	
Gets Results By Developing Successful Workers and By Building Influence in the Organzation	

In this chapter, you'll find useful information about:

The *what* of a manager's job (the two essential functions of a manager).

How a successful manager accomplishes these functions (Phase One and Phase Two Management).

The *payoff* for successful management.

A successful manager sees that the work assigned to his workgroup gets done. Here's how he does it.

D oes the title make it sound as though this chapter is going to be complicated and involved? It's not. Everything in it can be summarized in a few short sentences:

If you're a manager, the *what* of your job is to

1. See that your workgroup gets its assigned work done on time, in sufficient quantity, and with high quality; and

2. Do this in such a way that your boss is kept out of trouble and spends a minimum amount of time concerned with your workgroup.

The *how* of your job is accomplished in two phases:

In *Phase One Management*, you develop successful workers.

> **More than anything else you can do, developing successful workers is the key to being successful as a manager.**

Then, when you're successful in Phase One, you have time for *Phase Two*. In this phase, you

1. Develop influence with other managers and significant people,
2. Have the time and skills to perform special projects for your boss, and
3. Perform effectively as a manager responsible for self-managing teams.

When both Phase One and Phase Two are done successfully, this is the *payoff*:

1. You have a skillful and confident workgroup,
2. You're a successful member of your boss's workgroup,
3. You're extremely useful to your organization, and
4. You're promotable.

> In other words, the best way to get the workgroup's work done is also the way that benefits your workgroup, your boss, your organization, and yourself the most!

Sound too good to be true? It isn't. Read on and see.

MANAGING IS MANAGING

If you've read carefully to this point, you may have noticed that what a manager does sounds suspiciously like what a "supervisor" does. Congratulations! You win the door prize.

Supervision is management, and all management requires supervision. When you become a supervisor, you become a manager. You cross an invisible, critical line. This is the line:

> When you're a worker, whether a janitor or an attorney, you're responsible only for what *you* produce. When you become a manager, you become responsible for the completion of work that only *others* can accomplish.

From now on, if you are successful it will be because you are able to get others—your workgroup—to accomplish their assigned work. Your workgroup may be six shipment clerks or the vice-presidents of an international bank. It makes no difference; your first function as a manager is to see that the work assigned to your group is done, done right, and done on time.

If you're a new manager, it means that you've probably moved into a position called "first-level supervisor." That's a common title for the job, but don't let it hide the fact that you're really a manager now. For the rest of the book, this position will be referred to as "first-level manager"—to make it clear that you've crossed the line into management.[1]

---

[1]I asked a friend of mine who's a first-level manager to read the outline of this book. When he came to this point, he wrote in the margin: "Becoming a supervisor should not be considered the first level of management, but should be considered as the backbone of the management team." He's right, but you can be both.

SUCCESSFUL MANAGING: PHASE ONE

Traditionally, a first-level manager's basic function is to see to the completion of things that only others can accomplish. Just what does that mean? Let's see if we can flesh it out a bit by looking at one manager who's basically succeeding and one who's not doing so well.

George has been a first-level manager in the bindery of a printing plant for four years now. He's one of the hardest workers in the plant, always coming in early and staying late. Because he can't get workers with the skills he wants, he often does the more complicated work himself. Even when he doesn't have to do the whole job, he frequently has to step in and perform a difficult step for a worker. George makes it a point, though, to explain to the worker that he's not expected to be able to do the work—so he won't feel badly about George having to do it.

George believes he should get to know each worker and often stops to chat with them. He tries to find out what's important to them in their personal lives and asks about such. He avoids getting too chummy with them, though, since he often has to reprimand them for failing to do their work properly. In fact, he often complains to his wife about the time he has to spend chewing workers out and doing their work over.

Because of the importance of George's function and because his workforce isn't as good as he would like, George reports to his boss each morning on what the group accomplished the day before. George's boss will often come by once or twice a day, just to see how things are proceeding and to see if George needs help.

Susan has been the other first-level manager in the bindery for about the same length of time, but she has a very different style of managing. She's generally a quiet person who doesn't make small talk with her workers and insists that they call her "Mrs. Evers." She will occasionally pitch in to help her workgroup if they get behind schedule, but insists that otherwise, they do even the hardest work themselves. George thinks she's lazy because she almost never puts in extra time. And she makes a worker do a task over and over until it's done correctly, rather than going ahead and doing it herself.

Instead of spending time checking her people's work to see that it's done right, Susan often leaves her work area entirely and goes to chew the fat with other managers. George gets angry that she can get away with this, and wonders how she managed to get workers so much more reliable than his. It also makes him angry that her group so often gets preferential treatment from other departments.

On the other hand, Susan's boss doesn't spend much time with Susan or her people; most of the time, Susan has to go see her boss. Yet, Susan's boss often picks her to do special projects. George thinks it's unfair that Susan gets rewarded even though she doesn't spend enough time managing her people.

Neither manager is perfect, but have you picked the better one? It's Susan, of course. Were you surprised? The fact of the matter is that she is doing a much better job than George of performing a manager's two basic functions (the *what* of the job):

1. Susan sees that her workgroup gets its assigned work done on time, in sufficient quantity, and with acceptable quality. You or George might not agree with her methods, but they're working.
2. She does this in a way that keeps her boss out of trouble and allows him to spend the least possible time dealing with problems caused by her unit. That's why her boss comes by so seldom; he doesn't *need* to keep close tabs on her.

To understand George and Susan better, look critically at some of the things they do:

George puts in lots of time; he comes to work early and stays late. He has to put in these extra hours because he's doing so much of the work himself. George isn't getting work done *through* others—he's getting work done *instead* of them. His method takes time away from other things he should be doing. Even worse, it keeps each of his workers from learning the full job and taking responsibility for it. (He reinforces this when he points out to workers that they're not expected to be able to do the most difficult work.)

Susan communicates something very different to her people. She'll occasionally pitch in to help them, but she doesn't monopolize the hard (and often, most challenging) work. Instead, she insists that each worker do *all* of an assigned job, even the most difficult parts. When a worker makes a mistake, she has *him* do it over; that way, the worker learns how to do it right. Then Susan doesn't have to put in extra hours doing the work herself.

The fact that George wants to get to know each worker is one of his strong points, just as Susan's lack of contact with her group may handicap her. But making friends with their workers isn't an essential part of George's and Susan's jobs; it almost never makes or breaks a supervisor.

George also spends lots of time reprimanding his workers for not doing their jobs properly. As you'll see later in this book, the need to repeatedly guide a worker is a sign of a problem. It's not a normal part of management.

You can tell George isn't succeeding because his boss is spending so much time with him and his workgroup. Unless they happen to be bored or like their company, bosses don't spend a lot of time with their successful subordinate managers. They also don't like to spend time following up on work that's the responsibility of the subordinate manager. And they almost never "help" successful managers.

HOW A SUCCESSFUL MANAGER DOES IT

The next chapter describes a successful worker, and the chapters after that explain what a manager has to do to develop successful workers. If you look at the brief description of Susan's workgroup, though, you can catch a glimpse of what successful workers are like.

First of all, they're able to do even the most difficult work themselves. Second, they're reliable; they do the work without anyone looking over their shoulders. That's a lot right there—but the next chapter will show that it's just part of the total picture.

The important point to remember for now is that the way to get your workgroup's work done is to develop your workers into *successful* workers—and your workgroup into a successful workgroup. You don't do the work yourself; you don't force them to do it by over-managing them; and you don't just let them do it however they please. You start with the best people you can hire, and you develop them into successful workers.

Many books concentrate on the *activities* of a manager—what you do everyday. This one does, too. It describes structuring, selecting, guiding, correcting, motivating, delegating, and supporting—all of the things you have to do to develop successful workers. Remember, though, it's the *results* that count:

People in the organization care very much about the results of
your Phase One Management—about getting your *function* done
successfully. Few people, if any, care about the activities you do
to develop successful workers. In other words, you are free to
spend as little time as possible on Phase One Management, as long
as you produce the right results.

SUCCESSFUL MANAGING: PHASE TWO

Being good at Phase One Management isn't good enough. Look at
Susan again. Because her workgroup is successful, she has time to spend
doing other things outside her workgroup. She can build her influence
with other managers and other people on whom she has to rely. (That's
why she gets "preferential treatment.") She also has time to do special
projects for her boss. Because of this, her boss and other people that
matter think she's promotable.

Actually, that is a separate level of management—Phase Two Management. It's all of the things a manager does to develop influence
with other managers and with his boss. It's the time Susan spends
working with her peers and doing special projects for her boss.

Your first reaction may be that this is self-serving, something done
just to promote your own career. It does promote your career, but that's
not the only reason you do it. In fact, it's not even the main reason.

Chapters 16 and 17 talk more about Phase Two Management. All
that needs to be said about it here is this:

1. All workgroups depend on other groups to be successful. For
instance, isn't it much easier to do a job if the people who want it done
will work with you—instead of just criticizing when something's done
wrong? Isn't it much easier if the supplies you need arrive on time?
Good relations with other workgroups can accomplish this.

2. What you can do to develop successful workers depends greatly
on what your boss thinks of you. If he sees you as barely competent,
you'll never be given the freedom to help your workgroup become
successful. If he thinks you and your workers are competent and dedi-
cated, you'll have room to succeed.

3. How much influence a manager has over his workgroup de-

pends on how much influence the workgroup thinks he has on other managers and on his boss. If the workers think their manager has "clout," they'll do what he wants. If they don't, they probably won't.

ONE MORE TIME . . .

The functions of a manager (the *what*), the means a successful manager uses to become successful (the *how*), and the *payoff* from them hold true for all management jobs. It doesn't matter whether the workers are cashiers or fashion designers, supply clerks or nuclear engineers, computer programmers or department heads.

Whatever kind of organization a manager is in, the two basic functions of management are the same:

1. Develop a workgroup that gets its work done, and
2. Do it in a way that requires your boss to spend a minimum amount of time worrying about it.

The means are the same:

1. Develop successful workers (Phase One Management), and
2. Develop and use influence with other managers and with your boss (Phase Two Management).

And the payoff is still the same:

1. You have a skillful and confident workgroup,
2. You're a successful member of your boss's workgroup,
3. You're extremely useful to your organization, and
4. You're promotable.

THE SKILLS MAXIMIZATION MODEL

"Skills maximization model"—sounds impressive, doesn't it? It describes the model of successful management outlined in this book: a way of managing that gives everyone involved the opportunity to develop and use skills to the maximum.

The model was presented in the front of this book. We've looked at the main components of it in this chapter. This is what we have so far:

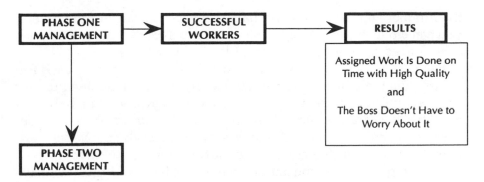

The next chapter will fill in more details by describing successful workers. But before you go on, you might want to use the first StretchMeter. What's that? Read on.

STRETCHMETERS AND ASAPS

At the end of most—but not all—of the chapters from now on you'll find "StretchMeters." A StretchMeter is a simple device with a simple function: it helps you evaluate whether, and how much, you need to "stretch" to master the skills described in that chapter.

There's nothing mysterious about a StretchMeter. It's a way for you to evaluate yourself quickly on a set of factors that are relevant to part of the first-level manager's job.

It's easy to use a StretchMeter. Each one has a series of statements describing a quality or a skill. Under each description is a range of numbers running from 0 to 8, that is, NEVER to ALWAYS. Here is an example:

I spend a great deal of time getting all of the details correct.

NEVER   0   1   2   3   4   5   6   7   8   ALWAYS

You use the StretchMeter by circling the number between NEVER and ALWAYS that best describes you. If you NEVER worry about the details, you would circle 0; if you ALWAYS spend a lot of time on them, you would circle 8. Most of the time, you'll probably circle a number somewhere between the two extremes.

The sample description above was a sample; it doesn't have a "right" answer where managing is concerned. From now on, the descriptions *will* have "right" answers. These answers are the ones represented by the numbers on the right-hand half of the range. Most of the time, if you can circle the 6 or the 7, you have as much of that quality or skills as you need to be a very effective first-level manager.

Each StretchMeter is made up of a series of descriptions, each followed by a scale like the one in the example. You circle one number on the line below each description. When you've finished that StretchMeter, draw a line connecting each of your circles. The closer the overall line is to the right-hand side of the scale, the better your overall score is for that cluster of qualities or skills.

What if part or all of the line is closer to the left-hand side? It means that you need to *stretch* on those qualities or skills in order to be really effective. That's where ASAP—"Adopting Stretching Actions Promptly"—comes in.

Each ASAP contains a set of actions that corresponds to the items in the StretchMeter. If you scored yourself low on Item #3 on the StretchMeter, use ASAP 3 to help you start developing that quality or skill.

You don't have to do the ASAP actions, of course—they're there simply to help you. Even if you do them, you won't be magically transformed overnight. But you will have taken the first step on an important journey.

Do you see the picture now? As you read this book and complete the StretchMeters, you'll begin to get an idea of your strengths and weaknesses. (If you didn't have strengths, you wouldn't be a first-level manager. If you didn't have weaknesses, you wouldn't be human.) Then you can choose the ASAP actions you want to do to start turning weaknesses into strengths.

One other thought: You might want to have a friend—someone you can trust to be honest with you—complete some of the StretchMeters on you, too. If the two of you come up with very different results (more than two numbers apart, for example), then you may want to ask yourself if you're really being objective. Or you may be right about yourself but don't always communicate what you're really like to others.

The first StretchMeter measures some of the personal qualities that it helps to have if you're going to be a good manager. None of them are absolutely necessary; in fact, there are good managers who lack some of them. On the whole, though, you'll do a better job (and do it more easily) if you have or develop most of these qualities.

To help you become used to Adopting Stretching Actions Promptly (ASAP), an ASAP has been included following this first StretchMeter. However, there is a basic difference between this meter and all other ones.

All other StretchMeters ask you to rate yourself on specific, limited skills. If you rate yourself toward the low end, it simply means you don't have the skill fully developed yet. The ASAP for that StretchMeter will get you started toward acquiring the skill.

This StretchMeter measures *qualities*—which are broad, deeply ingrained personal traits or characteristics. They reflect skills; for instance, the ability to approach tense situations objectively is a skill. However, they go much deeper than that, and acquiring them involves *unlearning* old behaviors.

For this reason, the short exercise presented in the first ASAP will barely scratch the surface. If you rate yourself below where you believe you should be in one or more qualities, you may want to look for a book or a course dealing with that specific quality—or perhaps try to learn from someone you respect who has that quality.

Don't give up or take a pessimistic attitude. Each of us can change very basic traits and qualities if determined to do it and willing to spend the effort. You should understand, though, that qualities do not change easily—and be prepared to invest the time and energy needed to make the change.

Enough talk—on to StretchMeter 1.

StretchMeter 1: DESIRABLE MANAGEMENT QUALITIES

1. I enjoy being with people.

NEVER   0   1   2   3   4   5   6   7   8   ALWAYS

2. I approach tense situations very objectively.

NEVER   0   1   2   3   4   5   6   7   8   ALWAYS

3. I can deal positively with frustrated people.

NEVER   0   1   2   3   4   5   6   7   8   ALWAYS

4. I enjoy helping other prople learn.

NEVER   0   1   2   3   4   5   6   7   8   ALWAYS

5. I'm comfortable letting others take the credit.

NEVER   0   1   2   3   4   5   6   7   8   ALWAYS

6. I can stay calm when someone interrupts me.

NEVER   0   1   2   3   4   5   6   7   8   ALWAYS

7. I can enjoy people who are different from me.

NEVER   0   1   2   3   4   5   6   7   8   ALWAYS

8. I prefer to act on my own, not wait to be told what to do.

NEVER   0   1   2   3   4   5   6   7   8   ALWAYS

9. Others will usually listen to me and do what I ask.

NEVER   0   1   2   3   4   5   6   7   8   ALWAYS

Desirable Management Qualities ASAP

1. One of the best ways to get to know your workers is also a good way to start enjoying being with them—share lunch or a break with them. For the next two weeks, plan to have lunch or a break with each worker in your workgroup at least once. You'll find plenty of reasons for not doing it, but don't let anything stop you. Do it. You may want to keep on doing it long after the two weeks are over.

2–3. A basic reason for reacting emotionally in tense situations or reacting negatively toward frustrated people is that the reaction "grabs" you before you have a chance to think. You need something to remind you not to react before you have time to think:

If you have a desk, find a simple object that doesn't belong there and place it in clear view. That object is now your official *Reaction Alert*. You're going to use it to remind yourself that you aren't going to react negatively. You're going to be calm and positive, no matter what. Every time you look at it, remember that. When someone comes in who's frustrated, use the object to remind yourself not to fall into your habitual negative response, and make a different response instead.[2]

If you don't have an office, or if you're often away from it, there's another method that often works. Carry around a small counter—such as the type that golfers use to record their scores. This is your portable Reaction Alert. Whenever you run into a frustrated individual and react negatively, punch the counter. It's remarkable how this will help you become aware of the problem.[3]

If neither of these sounds good to you, find another way. What you do doesn't matter. What does matter is that you find a reliable way to make yourself aware of your habitual reflex. Once

[2]To deal with a similar problem, I use an 8-inch green foam ball. It sits right in the middle of my desk. I've told my staff why it's there, so that we all know the situation we're trying to avoid. It works! (The idea, by the way, came from working with Merilee Zdenek, president of Right-Brain Resources in Reseda, CA.)

[3]This idea comes from a book called *Precision Nirvana* by Deane H. Shapiro, Jr. (Englewood Cliffs, NJ: Prentice-Hall, 1978).

you become aware of it, you gain the power to *choose* how to respond. Choosing is the name of the game.

4. One reason you may not enjoy helping other people learn is that you don't think of this as an important duty. You may think to yourself, "Oh, alright, I'll help him for a few minutes—then I'll get back to *my* job." If that's the case, you can manage this trait just by deciding that helping others learn *is* part of your job. It is. Helping others learn, or *guiding* them, is one of the seven critical activities of a manager. Don't wait until you read that chapter, though; decide now, *right now*, that helping people learn is important—and do it.

5. Letting other people take the credit can be very difficult for anyone. One reason is that you may be telling yourself that if someone else takes the credit, you can't have it. When you're a manager, that's not true; you get to take the credit for everything your workers do. So, within the next week, help at least two of your workers accomplish something (perhaps just get a task done on time or early) and then see that they get credit for it.

6. If you have trouble staying calm when interrupted, use the same technique given in ASAP 2—your Reaction Alert. A word of caution, though: *Don't* use the same reminder for two different purposes at the same time. In fact, you should deal with only one trait at a time, even if you rated yourself low in both. Get the first under control, then attack the second.

7. If you don't enjoy people who are different from you, you may have difficulty in managing them. As you get to know such people, their "differences" often fade away, and you can see them as just plain people. In the short run, you can use a Reaction Alert (see ASAP 2) and record each time you have stereotyped a person with your own negative reaction. That will at least make sure you're aware of your feelings—and that's a beginning.

8. As you'll see as you read this book, most of what a successful manager does is done on his own. In the next two weeks, find at least one small task a day that you can do without waiting for someone to tell you to do it. (The small task may be part of a larger task. For instance, if you want to wait until someone tells you it's okay to begin a new procedure, you can prepare all of the written copies of the procedure now to be handed out later.)

9. Having others listen to you and follow you is the mark of a leader—and you may not have thought of yourself as a leader before. There's no quick, easy way to become a leader. Unfortunately, becoming a manager doesn't make you one. If you practice Phase One and Phase Two Management conscientiously, though, you will become a leader.

A FINAL WORD

If you read the different ASAP items, you saw how many times a Reaction Alert could be useful. That's helpful learning right there. When you have trouble making a change you want to make, it's often because you make the habitual reaction before you realize it. You become aware of what you're doing *after* you've started to do it. Then it's usually too late to act differently.

The key is finding a way to become aware *before* you act. This is the purpose of a Reaction Alert. You'll find that some kind of Reaction Alert is one of the best aids you can have for effective change.

The two Reaction Alerts described previously actually work slightly differently. The one on your desk is designed to remind you *not* to react. The counter in your pocket probably won't do that. But it will let you tally up the number of times you reacted without thinking—and this will help you become aware of it.

You might find that something else works better for you. Go for it! The idea is to find something that will stop the reaction before it commits you to the behavior you want to change.

CHAPTER 2

The Successful Worker

SUCCESSFUL WORKERS	
Know What to Do	
Know How to Do It Well	
Have Tools to Do It Well	
Know When It's Done Well	
Are Motivated to Do It Well	
Take Responsibility for It	

In this chapter, you'll find useful information on the characteristics of a successful worker.

The goal of Phase One Management is to develop successful workers. This chapter describes what makes workers successful.

WHAT IS A SUCCESSFUL WORKER?

Elena Radice has been at Wendell Products since she graduated from high school three years ago. She started in the typing pool but moved to Accounts Payable two years ago. Although she likes accounting work, she's taking courses at night to become a paraprofessional.

In the meantime, she does her job well. She learned it from Harry Tomlin, the section supervisor. Harry worked closely with her for several days when she first started. He explained the system to her and showed her each of the formats that were used. Then he took her on a tour of the rest of the accounting department, to see how the data she input was used in the system as a whole.

The manual for the bookkeeping system worried her at first; it was very big and seemed quite complicated. Harry sat down and went through its basic structure with her. Then he gave her a group of transactions, showed her the chapter that described how to process them, and had her do them. When she had gotten them done correctly, he gave her a different group and showed her a different chapter. Before long, she knew how to do all of the routine transactions and where she could find the rules for the difficult ones.

While the manual was helpful, she soon found that it wasn't enough. Then Harry gave her some desk guides that other workers in the group had made up, and they were a great help. The workgroup had also developed worksheets for the most complicated transactions.

As soon as she was able to do a range of transactions, Harry explained her "responsibility code." At the beginning of the day, she typed her code into the computer. Then the code was added to every transaction she processed. "It lets you know if any of them have been done incorrectly," Harry explained. "If one of the transactions has to be returned because of an error, it comes right back to you to correct. I won't even know about it unless you make too many errors—then I'll get a printout, and I can help you figure out what's causing the mistakes." It wasn't long before Elena started to look at all the transactions she produced as "hers."

Elena wants to do a good job since she knows she will probably have to work for several years. The rest of the workgroup is conscientious, which helps. And whenever they have a particularly good day— very few errors—Harry posts the summary with "GOOD JOB!" on it in big letters.

Elena is good enough that she doesn't often have to ask others how to do a particular transaction, and she takes pride in seeing how long she can go without having one returned because of an error.

In other words, Elena is a good worker, who:

1. Knows what to do,
2. Knows how to do it well,
3. Has the tools with which to do it,
4. Knows when she has done it well,
5. Is motivated to do it well, and
6. Takes responsibility for it.

KNOWING WHAT TO DO

This sounds pretty obvious, doesn't it? Of course a worker should know what to do. But let's look at what can happen:

Van's boss calls him and tells him that the auditing department needs a report showing all the trips each auditor makes each month. Van identifies all the fields in the database that he needs and creates a complete report showing each auditor and the trips he made. (Van doesn't know that when the report gets to auditing, a secretary will make a list of the dates that auditors visited each location—which is the only information the auditing department really needs.)

Every morning John gets his priority orders out first. This takes extra time because a lot of stock for the routine orders is the same as that for the priority orders—which means he has to make two trips to the same area a lot of the time. But John was told that the priority stock needed to be picked first, and because he's conscientious, he tries to have all priority orders done and out the door by 9:00 A.M. (What the person who told him actually meant was that the priority orders must be ready to be picked up by 1:00 P.M.)

Jennie is responsible for drafting replies to congressmen who write letters to headquarters about the district office in which she works. She spends a great deal of time on each letter, making sure that she has each word just right. (She doesn't know that when the public relations office gets her letter, it is rewritten completely using a specific format.)

These examples illustrate how slippery "doing the right thing" can be. Jennie, John, and Van are all wasting time because they don't know why their work is done, or when it needs to be done, or what the people who need their work do with it.

They're all conscientious workers who want to do a good job. From their points of view, they *are* doing a good job. In reality, they're less productive than they could be, only because they haven't been told important particulars about their jobs.

Remember, knowing what to do includes:

1. Knowing *when* to do it,
2. Knowing *why* to do it, and
3. Knowing *what* the people you do it for (your customers) do with it.

Workers know what to do only if they receive effective guiding and correcting. Chapters 6 and 7 of the book cover this.

KNOWING HOW TO DO IT WELL

We all know how important training is. Workers can't do a good job if they don't know *how* to do it. But, if you want to succeed as a manager, just seeing that your people are trained isn't enough. You need to see that all of your workers know how to do their jobs *well*.

Here's a quick look at a workgroup where everyone knows how to do his job:

Ann produces very high quality reports, but it takes her a long time to do them. Jerry doesn't produce as good a report, but he can really whip them out. Oscar is a good solid worker, but he has a hard time getting reports out by their deadlines. Marie is the star; she produces good reports, does them quickly, and always meets her deadlines.

Your first reaction may be that, like all workgroups, this one is made up of individual workers, with individual differences. That's right, and it's an important point. But there's another way to look at it. Ann, Jerry, and Oscar know how to do their jobs. Marie knows how to do her job *well*.

Ann and Marie have a good sense of what makes a high quality report; they could probably teach this to the others. Jerry and Marie could probably show Ann and Oscar how to organize and execute their work efficiently and how to meet their deadlines. Then all four workers would know how to do the job well.

It's important that workers know how to do their jobs well, which includes doing quality work that's right the first time. This book will give a lot of attention to this, particularly in Chapters 6 and 7.

HAVING THE TOOLS TO DO IT WELL

This is something else that sounds very obvious. That doesn't mean it always happens:

> Sheri spends a lot of time sitting and waiting for her personal computer to compute. She has a really powerful machine, but the spreadsheet she uses is extremely slow. Since she does a lot of "what if" projections, she has to recalculate constantly. It sometimes takes a minute to do a recalculation, and she has to do dozens of them. She's asked for a faster spreadsheet program, but it doesn't look like she'll get one. It's organization policy to buy all software from the company that handles this spreadsheet in order to get a discount.

> Ed deals with computers in a different way—he helps manufacture them. Specifically, he attaches the last part to a hard disk drive and puts the drive on a conveyor belt. The procedures for his job say that he should put the drive on a cushioned pad before placing it on the belt. When there are pads there, Ed uses them. Otherwise, he just puts the drive on the belt. Since the pads aren't always there, he figures they can't be all that important. (He doesn't know that a drive that doesn't have a pad is three times as likely to fall off the belt and be damaged.)

As you can see, there are two parts to this point:

1. Having the right tools for the job,
2. Having them reliably at hand.

In the real world, one or both often get overlooked. Ed's company knew that a lot of its disk drives were being rejected, but it took several weeks to find out why. Sheri's organization still doesn't know how much of her time is wasted by using the wrong tool.

Chapter 10 deals with the importance of providing a constant supply of the right tools.

TELLING WHEN IT'S DONE WELL

"Mr. Augustine, how do I tell if I'm doing a good job?"

"No problem, Angelina. Around here, if no one is yelling at you, you're doing okay."

Does that sound like your experience? Have you worked in an organization whose basic performance information system was "No news is good news" (NNGN)? What was your reaction to it?

If Angelina is an experienced worker who is performing well—producing sufficient high-quality work on time—the NNGN feedback system will work. There really isn't much her manager needs to tell her. If her performance is below or above this level, though, she needs to know it—no matter how experienced she is.

If Angelina is a new worker, however, and not sure yet just what doing the job well *is*, *NNGN* is a lousy system. In this circumstance, she needs to know when she's meeting the standard just as much as she needs to know when she's performing above or below standard.

Some very sharp people have been known to say that the biggest single cause of low performance—even of experienced workers—is lack of this feedback. There's another problem: any worker who can't tell how well he is doing is at the mercy of the supervisor's opinion. Even if the supervisor is right, most workers really resent being in that position. That's why formal performance ratings are usually (1) a hassle and (2) inflated.

When a worker can tell how good a job he's doing, it increases that worker's control over his own work. For most workers, this leads to performance improvement—without anything else needing to be done. There are some very practical suggestions on how to create this situation later in this book, especially in Chapter 7.

MOTIVATED TO DO IT WELL

Edgar Miller was kicking off his quarterly management refresher course: "All right, I want each of you to list the three most serious problems you have on your job."

There was a flurry of paper shuffling and pencil scratching.

"Okay," he said. "Now, all of you who wrote down 'Motivating Employees' raise your hands."

All of the hands went up.

A manager has an impossible job if his workers don't care—and every smart manager knows this. There simply isn't enough time in the day to do everything else *and* try constantly to motivate workers, too.

"I just can't seem to motivate my workers," said the man in the pink shirt, who was sitting in the first row.

"Exactly," Edgar said.

A murmur went through the class. Edgar waited a moment, then said, "You can't motivate your workers. Either they motivate themselves, or they won't be motivated. Workers will always do what makes sense to them."

"Then why bother?" the man asked.

"That's simple. Your job is to arrange things for your workgroup so that what makes sense to them is doing the kind of job you want done."

This point is worth repeating and emphasizing:

People do what makes sense to them. If you want them to do their job well for you, make sure that doing it well makes sense and doing it poorly doesn't.

Here's a quick example of what this means:

Jonathan has moved into the city from a farm and taken a job with the state compensation office. He finds after only two months that he can easily process twice the average number of claims. As soon as he tries though, the other workers accuse him of "showing off." He tries a little longer, but it doesn't seem to matter to his boss. Now he processes just a little more than the average number and is looking for another job.

Jonathan has run into a double whammy:

1. He's being punished for doing well (his fellow workers criticize him for it), and

2. He and everyone else are rewarded for doing so-so work (because there's no reward for doing better).

Chapter 8 will give you ideas on how to avoid these whammies.

TAKING RESPONSIBILITY FOR IT

"Hey, Charlie, c'mon. We're waiting for you."

"Just a minute, Arnie. I don't have this solder joint right yet."

"Ah, let it go. One of the inspectors will catch it and send it back."

"Not on your life. In the first place, if an inspector catches it, he'll know it's mine. In the second place, it is mine—and I'm going to get the damned thing right."

Charlie understands what it takes to be a successful worker. If a worker knows what to do and how to do it, uses his tools effectively, knows when he's done a job well, and is motivated, that worker is still not successful until he takes responsibility for his work. Charlie takes pride in his work and takes responsibility for it, too.

When a worker takes responsibility for his work, it is done without intervention from you—unless he runs into something he doesn't understand. Otherwise, his work is done in the right quantity, in conformance with quality standards, and on time.

THE PAYOFF

One more time—a successful worker:

1. Knows what to do (and when to do it, why it is to be done, and what customers need from it),

2. Knows how to do it well,

3. Has the tools with which to do it,

4. Knows when he has done it well,

5. Is motivated to do it well, and
6. Takes responsibility for it.

When you have a workgroup made up of successful workers, the payoff for you is tremendous. As you go through this book, you'll see just how tremendous it is. Just as important, there's a tremendous payoff for the workers:

1. Because they're successful, they feel good about themselves, their workgroup, and their work.
2. Because they feel good about their work and each other, they can work closely together—as a team. This makes each individual even more successful, which makes the team stronger, which makes each individual more successful, . . .
3. Because they're successful—individually and together—they manage themselves. This gets them largely out of the boss-subordinate relationship that fewer and fewer workers *and* managers are comfortable with these days.*

Convinced? In the next chapter, you'll start learning the skills required to produce successful workers and a successful workgroup.

A BRIEF POSTSCRIPT

The rest of this book is about specific activities it takes for a manager to be successful. Don't forget, though, that a manager is a worker, too. You're part of your boss's workgroup. When you become a successful supervisor, by practicing successful Phase One and Phase Two Management, you will

1. Know what to do,
2. Know how to do it well,

---

*This is't a minor matter. Research data gathered by the McFletcher Corporation of Scottsdale, AZ, indicate that:
1. One-third of workers entering the work force don't want to be supervised, and
2. Three-fourths of current first-level managers would like to spend less time supervising.

3. Know what tools you need to do it well,

4. Know when you have done it well,

5. Be motivated to do it well, and

6. Take responsibility for it.

MORE OF THE SKILLS MAXIMIZATION MODEL

In the last chapter, several key components of the skills maximization model were described. This chapter added the characteristics of successful workers. Here are the parts of the model that have been described in this book so far:

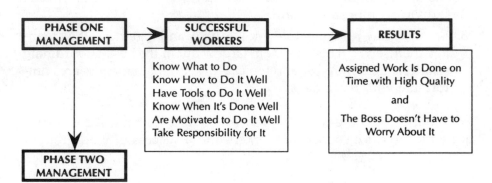

CHAPTER 3

Developing Successful Workers

PHASE ONE MANAGEMENT	
Structuring	C O M M U N I C A T I N G
Selecting	
Guiding	
Correcting	
Motivating	
Delegating	
Supporting	

In this chapter, you'll find overall information on the Phase One activities required to develop successful workers:

Structuring,

Selecting,

Guiding,

Corecting,

Motivating,

Delegating, and then

Supporting them.

You'll also find that good communication skills are essential for all of these activities.

This chapter presents a brief overview of the seven activities and the communication skills required to be a successful first-level manager.

A BRIEF CONVERSATION

"Good morning, Mr. Sugeno."
"Good morning, Shirley. Welcome to your first day as a first-level manager."

"Thanks. I think I'm ready for it."

"I'm sure you are. Have you had a chance to look at that survival manual for new managers that I gave you last week?"

"I won't pretend I've read it all, but I have looked at the first of it."

"Good—that's really what I'm concerned about. Since you're starting as a new first-level manager, I'd like you to be familiar at least with the basic activities of Phase One Management."

"Whew! At least I got that far."

"Would you tell me what these activities are? Don't worry about quoting the book; just put them in your own words."

"Let me see. There are seven of them, right?"

Mr. Sugeno nodded.

"I remember the first one—it's *structuring*. Structuring means planning and organizing the work flow and setting priorities so there are no delays due to confusion within the workgroup. Planning means anticipating workload and being ready for it; organizing means deciding who's going to do what; setting priorities means deciding which tasks are the most important. If you do these right, the workgroup knows *what* they have to do, *how* it needs to be done, and *when*."

"Excellent," Mr. Sugeno said. "Which reminds me that I have some details about next month's workload that I need to discuss with you and the other section chiefs. We'll do that later; right now, tell me about activity 2."

"The second activity is *selecting*, and I already know how important that is. I can see how quickly I'll get into trouble if I don't find workers who are able and willing to do the work, or if my workers aren't adaptable to the work and the workgroup. I'm lucky; Mrs. Winston was good at this, and she left me a good workgroup."

Mr. Sugeno smiled. "I'm counting on you to prove I'm good at it, too. Anyway, on to activity 3."

"The third one is . . . oh yes, the third one is *guiding*. After you've got workers selected, you have to see that they know what to do and how to do it. I can see from my own experience that an important part of knowing what to do is knowing *when* to do it, *why* it's done, and *who* you're doing it for. You know, when I first started here, it took me a year and a half to find out why I was doing the monthly summary. When I found out, I was amazed at how many different ways it's used."

Mr. Sugeno started to say something, but Shirley kept going: "The next activity is *correcting*, and I remember it because it fits right in with guiding. It's an important idea for me, because I've always thought of correcting as criticizing—and I don't like to criticize people. Now I understand that correcting is really giving useful feedback to people, and I feel better about it. I just hope I can get my workgroup feeling that good about it."

"I think you can. I'd suggest that you start by getting to know your people and letting them know what you expect. After you've been in the job a few weeks, I'm sure I'll hear what their first reactions are, and I'll be glad to share them with you. Anyway, we're up to activity 5, aren't we?"

"Yes, and I suppose that it's the one that sounds the hardest to me. *Motivating* other people just sounds difficult. It did help me some when I read that my job isn't really to motivate them but to create an environment, a job structure, and a reward system that motivates them. That sounds like something I can do, even if it does take me awhile."

"You can, and it probably will. Keep in mind that we pay a bonus to any workgroup that beats its monthly quota by 20 percent—and the supervisor gets part of the bonus. For now, though, tell me about activity 6."

"That's *delegating*, and it's going to be something brand new for me. Effective delegating means that I give each worker the most complete delegation he can handle at that moment. The goal is for me to develop my workgroup to the point where the workers can do their jobs without me looking over their shoulders. Each delegation should stretch them a little, but I need to be realistic and not delegate more than they can handle. I expect to find this quite challenging."

"It is. Why don't you keep some notes on what you've delegated to each of your people, and let's get together Friday at nine o'clock to go over it. I hope you understand that this is just temporary. It won't be long before I'll leave those decisions completely up to you. Now, tell me about activity 7."

"That's *supporting* my people. It means letting them do their jobs and backing them up when they do—even if they do their work differently than I would have done. I can remember a couple of times when I made decisions and my boss didn't back me up—it was painful for me. I'm certainly going to try to give my workers the training and the tools they need, and then stay out of their way and let them perform. I hope I can count on you to come talk to me if you think one of my people has goofed up. After all, I'm the one who'll delegate the responsibilities to them, so I'm the one you should chew on."

"I see you understand a lot about supporting your people already. You let me know if any of the other section chiefs give you a hard time, and I'll talk to them. I wouldn't have picked you for this job if I didn't think I could rely on you to give me your best. We've gone over the seven activities, but isn't there something we've left out?"

"Yes, but it isn't really an activity. It's *communication*. Good communication skills are what make it possible for a manager to do the seven activities effectively. This part of the manual really surprised me. I thought it would start off by talking about persuasion skills, but they came last. It said that it is more important for a manager to be open and honest; to be able to speak and write clearly; to listen responsively; and to give and seek feedback. If I can do all that, it won't take much more for me to be very effective at persuasion."

"I think you will be, too. Frankly, I was a little concerned about the short time you've been with us when I selected you for the job. As I listen to you, though, I hear some real enthusiasm and forcefulness in your approach. I'm convinced that you'll fit in well with our management style here. Let's see if you really remember what you've told me. Quickly, now, what are the seven activities?"

"Structuring, selecting, guiding, correcting, motivating, delegating, and supporting. And before you ask, the basis for doing all this effectively is good communication. How's that?"

"Excellent. Well, you'd better get in there and get to work."

"Yes, I'd better. Oh, here's your book back."

"From what you said, I thought you liked it."

"I do—so I bought my own copy."

"I'm glad I loaned it to you. Before you go, though, tell me where I can read about the seven activities and good communication skills."

"Oh, that's easy. The next eight chapters tell all about them."

CHAPTER 4

Structuring

PHASE ONE MANAGEMENT	
Structuring	C
Selecting	O
Guiding	M
Correcting	M
Motivating	U
Delegating	N
Supporting	I
	C
	A
	T
	I
	N
	G

In this chapter, you'll find useful information on:

> What effective structuring is and why it's important for success as a manager.
>
> How to plan work.
>
> How to organize work.
>
> How to set priorities.
>
> How to handle required programs.

Structuring will not directly help you develop successful workers. However, when you effectively structure the work of your workgroup, everyone is able to concentrate on doing his job successfully.

WHAT IS EFFECTIVE STRUCTURING?

Perhaps Eula Jefferson learned the importance of getting organized while she was a secretary for five years. Or perhaps it was while she held down a job, raised two boys, and went to night school to finish her degree. Whenever it was, she learned it well.

The managers who work with her keep asking what her secret is. She laughs. "There isn't any secret," she says. "It's just getting things arranged so my people and I aren't the bottleneck."

She certainly does that. As soon as she finds out that a project is coming their way, she calls a "skull session" with her workgroup. (She picked up that term from her football-playing sons.) Together she and the group make their best estimate of the time the project will take. She looks at the schedules for their other projects; if it looks like there will be a time conflict, she makes notes to discuss the problem with her boss and get it resolved.

When she sees that the workgroup's scheduling will permit them to take on the new project, they start to work out who will do it. Sometimes one worker can do the job alone; other times, it takes several working together. They agree on the critical milestones for the project. If it's going to be done by a group of workers, Eula makes sure that every person in the group knows who will do what.

When the project arrives, the workgroup is prepared for it. They know what to do and who will do it. As Eula likes to say, "If you've done your planning and organizing and set your priorities, the execution's a snap." (She picked that phrase up from her sons, too.)

WHY IS EFFECTIVE STRUCTURING IMPORTANT?

Eula's boss can answer that one for you:

"The gentleman who headed the section before Eula took over was a whiz in the field, but he just wasn't any good at structuring his workgroup. When a new project hit the group, he and the workers would run around in circles trying to figure who was going to do what. When he tried to assign it to various people, they'd all tell him that they were already working on another hot project that had to get done. Once he finally got the new work assigned, not only would it end up being behind schedule, but it would make another two or three projects late along with it.

"Everybody in the section really liked him, but he drove them nuts every time a new project came along. It's the difference between night and day since he got a transfer and Eula took over the job. Now I can count on getting their work on schedule, and they probably produce 20 percent more than they did before Eula stepped in. There hasn't been much change in personnel. It's just that they all know what they're doing and what they're going to do."

HOW DO I STRUCTURE EFFECTIVELY?

There are three aspects of structuring: *planning, organizing,* and *setting priorities*. None of them is any more important than any other, but planning is the first step.

Planning

Arnold Svensen has spend a lot of time learning about planning. Now he's an expert at it. Sometimes he knows when a heavy workload is going to hit his group, and sometimes he doesn't. He's learned how to be prepared either way. Here are some of the things he and his people do:

1. They gather all of the intelligence they can about what's happening "upstream," in the part of the organization where their workload originates. Arnold spends a few hours every week talking with managers involved with work that may come to him. That way, he always has some idea of when new work will arrive—even if he hasn't heard anything officially. He encourages his people to keep *their* eyes and ears open, too. He can't prevent every surprise, but he comes close.

2. Arnold stays abreast of the status of all the work in his group. That way, when new work comes in he doesn't have to go find out when his people will have time for it. He pays particular care to jobs that are slipping or are ahead of schedule, so they don't catch him by surprise either. Because his people have learned how important planning is, they keep one another up-to-date as well.

3. Arnold insists on being realistic when he plans out a job. He has a reputation for being "hard-nosed," but to him it's just being practi-

cal. Things almost never go as well as they could, and he allows room for delays. The managers who gripe at him because he gives realistic dates also know that he will deliver when he says he will. (In fact, he has a sign on his wall that says "Underpromise and Overdeliver"* and every so often he lectures his workgroup on it.)

4. Finally, Arnold always makes plans, but he never lets his group or his boss "fall in love" with them. He's seen too many situations where plans were set in concrete. When something happens that disrupts the plans, everybody gets uptight and has to let off a lot of steam before they can get on with the work of making the changes. He stresses to his workgroup that a plan may be what they use for now, but when conditions change, the plan changes too. That way, the group knows where it's going but stays light enough on its feet to change quickly.

EXAMPLE: Effective Planning

Now that Arnold knows for sure when the Western project is coming in, he meets with his three senior workers.

First, he describes the project to them and gives them a chance to ask questions. When this is over, they all know the basic requirements of the project. Arnold has also made a list of several important questions that need to be answered.

Then Arnold has each worker review for the group the status of his most important jobs. Arnold summarizes on the blackboard what each one says. When they finish this step, they all have a good idea about where the new project can be fitted in.

Arnold then assigns the project to Evelyn. Since adding the new project overloads her, he transfers another project from her to Howard. Then he asks Ben to work on specific parts of the project with Evelyn.

He leaves the last step to Ben and Evelyn—designing the basic plan. He gives them two days to come up with:

1. A description of each important step, and
2. The date when each step will be completed (the "milestones" for the project).

*Copied, no doubt, from Tom Peters' book, *Thriving on Chaos*. (New York: Alfred A. Knopf, 1987). See "How to Create Your Own Management University" at the end of this book.

When Evelyn gets back to him with the plan, he approves it as they wrote it, with one exception. They don't expect to have the first action completed until six weeks after the start. Arnold is uncomfortable waiting this long to be sure they're "on track," so he asks them to give him an interim report after three weeks. The basic planning is now complete.

(**WHAT IF** Arnold's workgroup weren't sufficiently advanced to share in the planning to this extent? How might he have done the basic planning—but still involved at least some workers in a way that would help them learn to plan?)

Organizing

"It doesn't do a lot of good to plan if you don't get things organized so you can carry the plan out." That's what Betty Rigelski would tell you. "Organizing means taking your plans and seeing that they go as you expect them to. These are some of the things it takes:

"First of all, you have to have a good plan. If it's unrealistic, too optimistic, or based on bad information, no amount of organizing will save you. At my previous job we'd get our projects in big batches. My manager wanted to make everybody happy, so he'd promise things we couldn't deliver. We'd juggle jobs all over the place and still end up late. If you start with a poor plan, you're going to end with screwed-up organization.

"The second thing is that you have to have the right people doing the right things. If you had the perfect organization, everybody would be great at all the jobs. But in reality, you know that it works better if certain people take certain parts of the job. I think it's because they feel that particular steps are 'their kinds of jobs,' and they put more of themselves into such tasks. (I do try to get the person who is particularly good at something to show the others how to do it well.)

"Of course, you have to be careful here, too, or people will get burned out or stereotyped. I try to make sure that everybody gets a chance at some of the most difficult work and that everybody gets some variety.

"So you start with a good plan, and you give it to the right people. Then you have to make sure that you're on top of things. I don't bug my people with a bunch of formal reports, and I don't keep asking them how things are going. I do make sure they give me a status report as often as necessary. And they know to tell me if they get ahead of or behind schedule. That way, I don't get any surprises. They know that while I trust them to do the work, I still care about it. And when one of the summaries is due, they have to stop for a minute and see just where they are.

"I guess the last thing about organizing is the most important: Everybody concerned with a job needs to know just who's going to do what. It took me a long time to learn what this means. "When I started out as a first-level manager, I took this idea literally. I thought about every detail and made sure I assigned it to someone. I gradually found out how wasteful this was; some of my people would have nothing to do while others were working their heads off. Worst of all, I'd ask about something, and someone would say, 'That's Charlie's job—ask him.'

"From there I went to the other extreme. I'd get a team together and give it the project. Then I'd tell the members to get it done however they wanted. Sometimes this worked, and I still use it when I have the right team. Many times it didn't work, and important things wouldn't get done because each member of the team thought someone else was doing them.

"I guess I'm somewhere between those two extremes now. I make sure that the team identifies all the major tasks and that it has a system for seeing that each one gets done. Several teams have started making up a checklist of all the tasks on a job. The members meet every so often—depending on the job—to see that someone is handling each task. This way nothing falls through the cracks, and they can trade tasks around to balance out people's workloads."

EXAMPLE: Organizing

Betty was true to her first requirement: As soon as she knew the date of the office move, she developed a realistic plan for it. She had to have the plan first in order to organize effectively.

Because Betty's people are used to working together, she lets them decide who will do the project. She reserves the right to make the final choice, but the appropriate individuals volunteer and she selects them. In fact, one of the people whom she wants to get experience in this kind of work asks to be on the team.*

The next step is to discuss any possible major problems and how they might be handled. This lets Betty tell her group at what point she wants to be notified that a problem is developing. ("If Supply thinks it will have trouble getting us the cartons, let me know right away.") Betty also reminds her workers to let her know about any schedule changes—so she can work them into their overall planning.

Since the team's leader is inexperienced in leading a team, Betty has him give her a list of the major tasks, showing who will do them. The two of them go over the list to make sure that someone has been assigned to each important job. Betty suggests to the leader that he get the team together every two weeks just to make sure that everyone agrees on who's doing what.

Then she turns the project over to the team.

(**WHAT IF** the person whom Betty wanted to get the experience hadn't volunteered? How could Betty have gotten that worker onto the team without forcing him?)

*Have you noticed that picking the people for the team has shown up under planning *and* organizing? For good reason: Most of the time, planning and organizing overlap each other. (This is particularly true when it's done with or by the workers involved.) In a book, we can say, "This is planning" and "That is organizing." In the real world, they're much harder to separate—and they don't need to be separated to be done effectively.

(You've probably guessed that the same is true for setting priorities—it's part of planning and organizing.)

Setting Priorities

Setting priorities is another aspect of structuring. Most workgroups receive more projects than they can handle in the time available. To succeed, they have to finish the important jobs first and do the rest as time permits.

Raymond Bernstein thought his workgroup was having trouble setting its priorities. He called an informal staff meeting, and this is what he told them:

"First of all, I want each one of you to understand that there's a big difference between 'pressing' and 'important.' A job that's pressing is one that needs to be completed soon—but it may or may not be important. There are also jobs that are important, and they may or may not be pressing. Sometimes it's easy to put off working on an important job because a less important one is pressing. Don't do it unless you're sure that the important one will still get done on schedule.

"Second, no priority is cast in cement—even if I'm the one who set it. If I give you a job and a deadline that you think will make you miss a more important deadline, you need to tell me this *right away*. Then we can decide which project is more important, and I can defend the decision to my boss if necessary.

"Third, never change a priority or deadline at the last minute unless you have a very good reason. If I give you a deadline on something and you come to me the day it's due and say you won't have it done because something more important came up—you're in trouble. It's true, I said you can always negotiate with me if you think a priority's date is unrealistic, but you do this up front, not the day the work is due.

"Finally, you should always know what your most important job is, and that's the job you should be doing. You can always find a few piddling jobs lying around, and every so often you have to do some cleaning up. You can take a little time for this, but make sure you don't make it a priority.

"Let me close with a word of wisdom. The difference between an outstanding worker and a so-so worker is not the fact that they do the *same* things but the outstanding worker does them better. Actually, the outstanding worker does *different* things. Most of the time, this means that he does the most important things—while the so-so worker spends a lot of time on less important things. I want you all to be outstanding workers."

EXAMPLE: Setting Priorities Effectively

Ray calls Kim, one of his newer workers, into his office. "Kim, I want you to take this report and rework the figures in it—using this month's totals. I need it by tomorrow afternoon."

"I can do that, but I'll have to let the cost report slide another day. I'm supposed to have it out on Friday, and if I lose a day, I can't make it."

"Hmm, that is a bind."

"Mr. Bernstein, I know how the cost report is used. What are they going to do with this report?"

"Good—I was hoping you'd ask that. Mr. Dubois wants to see how we did this month."

"They need the cost report plan for next month. Shouldn't I get it done first and then do this revision? I can have the revision for you sometime Monday."

"You're sure you can get it done Monday?"

"Pretty sure. If I can't, I can let you know tomorrow. Is that okay?"

Yes. I'll let Mr. Dubois know we expect to have it for him Monday."

(**WHAT IF** Kim had just agreed to do the job for Ray without asking questions?)

STRUCTURING IN REQUIRED RESPONSIBILITIES

"Dammit, Marge, managing today isn't what it was when I started! We didn't have to worry about EEO and OSHA and hazardous materials and all that garbage. We could concentrate on what we get paid for—getting the production out."

"I didn't think things were really that bad."

"Well, they are. I try to get the work out, and some turkey comes by and tells me I ought to hire more minority workers. No sooner do I get back to work when someone else comes by and asks me when was the last time I checked to see that everybody was wearing safety shoes and what we do with the used cleaning fluid. Then another joker from the head shed wants to know if I've talked with everybody about the Employee Assistance Program. By the time I get them off my back, the day's over."

"I'm sorry to hear that. I guess things must be different in your section. I try to take these programs in stride and work them along with my regular workload."

"What do you mean, 'work them with your regular workload'?"

"Well, whenever someone tells me I've got to support some new program, I give it the old one–two–three–four."

"The old what?"

"The old one–two–three–four:

1. I find out all I can about the program right away. I want to know how it applies to my people and what we do. That way I can figure out how much impact it'll have.

2. I think about how I can make the program work for me. For example, I've been using EEO for months to get personnel to look harder for better candidates for me. If I'm going to support something, I want it to work for me—not against me.

3. Once I understand a new program and what my role is, I make it a part of what I do. When the company put in that Employee Assistance Program, I went over it in a couple of group meetings and I made it one of the things I talk about with people during their appraisals. That's how I found out that one of my people was terribly worried about his daughter. I got him into the program, and now his performance is 100 percent improved.

4. If some program starts getting in our way, I make sure my boss knows about it. I don't make excuses for avoiding the program, but I make sure he knows that it's having a negative impact on morale or productivity or whatever. When they sent out that letter about sexual harassment on the job a few months ago, my guys were almost afraid to talk to the women in the group. Well, I said something to the boss, and he talked to the front office, and they sent out that second letter. My people are still a little uneasy, but at least they can talk about it now.

"Anyway, that's my old one–two–three–four. (1) I find out about the program; (2) I make it work for me; (3) I make it a part of what I do on the job; and (4) I let people know if it starts to get in the way. I tell you, it works."

"Ah, you're lucky, Marge. Besides, you're a woman and they treat you differently anyway. Two more years and you can have this place. . . . "

EXAMPLE: Using Required Programs Effectively

When Marge took over her section, she knew she'd have to pay attention to EEO. Bill, who had had the section before her, had told her that he'd been constantly hassled to hire more minorities. Bill also told her that he would have done so, if he could have found qualified candidates.

One of Marge's first trips was to talk to the EEO manager to make sure she understood how the program worked. Then she made a trip to the Human Resources office to find out exactly how recruiting was handled.

As a result, she and Human Resources agreed that they would focus on finding qualified women and minority group candidates for her to consider whenever she had a vacancy. She also made sure that Human Resources knew she was serious and not just going through the motions.

Because of this action, the EEO manager gave her some slack. Human Resources did its job, and when she filled her next five vacancies, she selected one woman and two male members of minority groups. She didn't do anything special—they were just well qualified and available and she picked them.

Marge has been in the job three years now, and no one has hassled her about EEO.

(**WHAT IF** the workgroup had been having too many accidents when Marge took over? What could she have done to start structuring safety into the way she managed?)

Why are we talking about required programs in this chapter? If you boil down what Marge said, it means "take these programs and *structure* them into your everyday managing." She planned for them, then organized the way they were used, and gave them the priority they needed. And that's what works.

A QUICK SUMMARY

Successful managers are effective at structuring their workgroups. They don't want to waste precious time fighting their workloads.

They *plan*, by:

1. Getting all of the intelligence they can so they're not surprised by a change in workload,
2. Keeping up with the status of all the work in their groups,
3. Being realistic when they plan, and
4. Never letting people "fall in love" with the specifics of their plans.

They *organize*, by:

1. Starting with a good plan,
2. Having the right people do the right things,
3. Knowing the status of a job at all times, and

4. Seeing that everyone concerned with the job knows who's going to do what.

They set *priorities*, by:

1. Knowing the difference between what's pressing and what's important,
2. Letting each worker question even the priorities they impose,
3. Not letting their workers wait until the last minute to change deadlines, and
4. Seeing that their people always know what their most important jobs are and that they work these jobs. (And they know that outstanding workers are often outstanding because they get their priorities straight.)

They deal with a required program, by:

1. Finding out about the program,
2. Making it work for them,
3. Structuring it into what they do on the job, and
4. Letting *their* managers know if the program starts to get in the way of their group's effectiveness.

StretchMeter 2: STRUCTURING

1. Before I make plans, I get all of the information I can.

NEVER   0   1   2   3   4   5   6   7   8   ALWAYS

2. My plans are realistic and practical.

NEVER   0   1   2   3   4   5   6   7   8   ALWAYS

3. My plans make it easy to organize the work.

NEVER   0   1   2   3   4   5   6   7   8   ALWAYS

4. When I organize a project, everyone knows what to do.

NEVER   0   1   2   3   4   5   6   7   8   ALWAYS

5. I can tell the difference between "pressing" and "important."

NEVER   0   1   2   3   4   5   6   7   8   ALWAYS

6. I don't let workers extend deadlines at the last moment.

NEVER   0   1   2   3   4   5   6   7   8   ALWAYS

7. My workers know what their most important jobs are.

NEVER   0   1   2   3   4   5   6   7   8   ALWAYS

8. I understand EEO, safety, and other special programs.

NEVER   0   1   2   3   4   5   6   7   8   ALWAYS

9. I structure these programs into my daily management.

NEVER   0   1   2   3   4   5   6   7   8   ALWAYS

10. I make EEO, safety, and so on work for me and my workgroup.

NEVER   0   1   2   3   4   5   6   7   8   ALWAYS

Structuring ASAP

Which number did you score yourself lowest on in the StretchMeter? Find the ASAP with the same number and do the ASAP starting tomorrow. (And it's okay to do more than one!)

1. Almost every effective management action is based on good information. Get all the facts you can about the next work your unit will get (it can be the morning's work, a new project, or an estimate of something weeks away). Write the information down and use it to plan how you'll handle the workload.

2–3. If your plans aren't realistic and practical, or if they don't make it easy to organize, they won't help much. Write a plan for how you'll spend your morning. Do you spend it that way? If not, plan the afternoon. Keep on planning until you come up with a realistic plan you can stick with; then continue planning every day until it becomes routine.

4. Assigning tasks is a basic part of organizing. Take a plan you're working on now or start a new plan. Write down every task that has to be done. Beside each task, write the name of the person who will do it. If more than one person will do it, identify the person with overall responsibility. See that the job is done that way. Then evaluate how effective you were and do better on the next one.

5. Other people often try to make you think that their pressing deadlines should be important deadlines for you. To be effective in your job, you need to know the difference. Make a list of your workgroup's priorities. Mark each one **P** (for pressing) or **I** (for important). If a task has to be done in the next week, but its completion won't affect your service to your customers or your boss, it's a **P**. If it *will* affect your service to them, no matter when it's due, mark it **I**. If it's an **I** that must be done in the next week, underline it. Do the underlined **I**'s now. Then start on the rest.

6. There is no excuse for deadlines slipped at the last moment, except simple sloppiness. Make it clear to your workers that— unless there is a real emergency—they cannot change a due date without at least three days' notice. (If three days isn't reasonable for your operation, pick a period of time that is.)

7. Workers should always know which tasks are the most important. Make a list of the jobs in your workgroup, in priority order. Talk with one of your most experienced workers and at least two of the least experienced ones. Ask them what their priorities are. If they aren't almost the same as yours, decide how to communicate more effectively starting today.

8. If you don't understand programs you're required to support, they'll keep getting in your way. Go to the EEO office, the safety office, the Employee Assistance Program office, or a similar office tomorrow morning. Ask the individual responsible for the program to explain how it can help you. Take at least one suggestion and implement it when you get back to your group. (If you can't go there, call.)

9. The way you use required programs effectively is to make them part of your daily managing. Sit down right now and choose at least one way you can use the EEO, safety, the Employee Assistance Program, or a similar program as part of your normal routine. Start doing it today.

10. How do you make required programs work for you? See ASAP 8.

CHAPTER 5

Selecting

PHASE ONE MANAGEMENT	
Structuring	C
Selecting	O
Guiding	M
Correcting	M
Motivating	U
Delegating	N
Supporting	I
	C
	A
	T
	I
	N
	G

In this chapter, you'll find useful information on:

What three characteristics the workers you select should have.

How to make effective personnel selections (including how to use interviews to your best advantage).

Why you need to be the kind of manager who will attract high-quality candidates for a job opening.

To develop successful workers, you must select individuals with the potential to be successful. The higher their potential, the less time and effort it will take to develop them.

WHAT IS EFFECTIVE SELECTING?

Henry Montoya is the envy of the other supervisors in the purchasing branch. Somehow he always gets the cream of the crop of new workers. They learn their jobs quickly, do them without a lot of supervision, and seem to enjoy working there.

It's not that Henry hasn't explained.

"Look," he says, "I put time into making my selections. I interview all of the candidates Human Resources will send me and I study them—carefully. If a person's going to work with us, I want that person to pass three tests:

"First, he has to be able to do the job, or at least be able to learn it quickly.

"Next, I look for motivation. I don't want someone who is going to want to do a good job only if I'm hanging over him all the time.

"Last of all, I look to see if he will fit in—which is really two things: One, I want someone who's going to be happy doing this kind of work day in and day out; and two, I want someone who's going to fit into the workgroup.

"If I can't find someone who can pass all three of these tests, I keep looking. When I do find someone, that's whom I hire. That's really all there is to it."

WHY IS EFFECTIVE SELECTING IMPORTANT?

Some supervisors do a "quick and dirty" job on their selections. Henry knows better. He knows that effective selecting is the basis for everything else he'll do with that worker.

He knows that a new person who doesn't have the right skills will require a lot of extra guiding and correcting.

He knows that a new person who isn't motivated will take extra guiding and correcting, even one who has the skills. Henry's had too much experience to believe that he can "motivate" just anyone. He also knows that it's very time-consuming even when such motivation is successful.

And he knows that a new person who doesn't fit the job and the workgroup, no matter how skilled and motivated he is, will get unhappy with the work sooner or later.

HOW DO I MAKE EFFECTIVE SELECTIONS?

Be Realistic

Always make the best selections possible. But be realistic.

Eleanor Downs is another supervisor who makes excellent selections. But she has a slightly different approach. If she's hiring from outside the organization, she knows her choices are limited by the organization's reputation, the quality of its pay and benefits, any competitors for employees, and a host of other influences she can't control.

It's not much different when she's hiring from inside. Here, she's limited by the selections other supervisors have made, the existing commitments the organization's workers have to it, career patterns, and similar elements that are beyond her control.

Eleanor knows she'll be selective, but she's realistic about how selective she can be. She always tries to get the best available workers, but she also knows she may have to compromise at some point and take someone who can't pass all three tests.

If she has to compromise, though, she knows it won't be on motivation. She looks for motivation first, and for the ability to fit in second. If a person passes those two tests, and has the native intelligence her work requires, Eleanor hires him—confident that he will be able to learn to do the job.

EXAMPLE: Realistic Selection

Eleanor learned the hard way about being realistic. Just after she was promoted into her current job, one of the engineers left. She recruited for his replacement for six months without finding someone who was just what she wanted. She finally gave up and took an individual with the right credentials but a poor work history.

Her new engineer was qualified on paper, but he certainly wasn't motivated to do a good job. After spending a lot of time trying to change his attitude, she finally decided to let him go. The day before she planned to tell him, he announced that he had a new job.

Fortunately, Eleanor learned two lessons from the experience. First, she wasn't going to be able to get a top candidate each time. Second, hiring someone who lacked the desire to do a good job was about the worst choice she could make.

She didn't solve the problem completely, but she found ways to reduce it. When the engineer left, she changed the position to that of technician. It turned out that the organization was competitive for technicians, and she hired a good one. In a few months, she had persuaded him to take advantage of the organization's tuition assistance program and begin work on an engineering degree at night.

In other words, she's become realistic about making the best selections possible under the circumstances.

(**WHAT IF** engineers suddenly became available on the job market? Should Eleanor keep trying to hire technicians? Remember, you pay technicians less than you pay engineers.)

Eleanor knows, too, about the risk involved in making a selection. There's always the chance that the person she picks won't live up to her expectations. Eleanor keeps polishing her selection skills—because she knows that the better she gets at selecting, the better her selections will be.

Gather Lots of Information

One way you keep your mistakes few and far between is to get and use lots of information on the candidates for your jobs.

Robert Stinson knows this, and his selections show it. When he has a job to fill, he takes the time and patience to get the information he needs. He looks at résumés, talks to people, interviews candidates. He knows it would be easier to just hire any candidate who will do. But Robert won't take the easy way out because he knows he'll pay for that mistake a dozen times over.

Instead, Robert concentrates on finding good information. He looks over résumés, evaluations, and any other papers carefully. He may talk with the Human Resources office about the candidates. But these aren't his main sources. When he really wants the straight scoop, he talks with:

1. The candidate's previous supervisors if he knows and trusts them, especially if they understand his kind of work; and

2. Current or past workers who know the candidate, particularly if they are (were) very good workers.

He's learned to be very suspicious of:

1. Appraisals or ratings that were prepared for the candidate to use for this job,
2. Written references the candidate brings with him (he knows that supervisors tend to give inflated appraisals of workers in both these situations,) and
3. The recommendations of current supervisors he doesn't know (some supervisors will try to "sell" a worker they want to get rid of or talk down a good worker they want to keep).

EXAMPLE: Getting and Using Information

Robert's care saved him on a recent selection. The Human Resources office sent him a carpenter who had a fine recommendation from her last company. Robert made a routine phone call to her last manager. Sure enough, the candidate's ex-boss was very high in his praise of the woman. He assured Robert that he'd hire her back at any time. When Robert asked if she were leadership material, the other man hesitated—but then assured him energetically that she was.

Robert had the feeling that he shouldn't stop there. He called the woman's manager from her next-to-last job and got a completely different picture. The woman was very competent, the manager said, but he had let her go because of carelessness. In fact, he told Robert, he had heard that she had just had to resign from a job for the same reason.

So, Robert kept on looking.

(**WHAT IF** Robert had told the carpenter he would hire her and then found out about her carelessness? What could he have done then?)

Beware of Your Hot (and Cold Buttons)

Pushing the "hot button" is a phrase salespeople use to describe positive emotional reaction from someone else says or does just the right thing.

Richard Feldman is a new manager who worries about his hot (and cold) buttons a lot. His first two employee selections turned sour on him. When he reviewed those decisions, he realized that he didn't look carefully enough at either person. Instead, he selected them because they both "seemed" right for the job.

Richard won't do that again. Like the rest of us, he was provided with a generous supply of hot and cold buttons as he was growing up. Now, though, Richard is aware that his buttons were pushed by the people he selected. They appealed to him because they looked like "clean-cut, solid Americans;" perhaps they were, but they turned out to be lousy workers.

Richard has made it a point to get to know and understand his *stereotypes* (another word for hot and cold buttons), and to keep people from using them to manipulate him. Now when he sits across the table from a "clean-cut, solid American," he makes sure that he looks beyond the person's front.

It's paid off for him, too. His third selection was beginning to go the way of the first two, until he asked himself some tough questions. In the end, he selected a minority woman candidate—Velma Thompson—the first woman in his workgroup. She turned out to be one of his best workers.

(Richard had always prided himself on not being discriminatory. If he didn't have any women in his workgroup, he had told himself, it was because none of them had been "well-enough qualified." It shook him to realize how close he had come to deciding that Velma wasn't qualified.)

EXAMPLE: Hot and Cold Buttons

Richard wasn't alone in making mistakes because someone pushed his "hot buttons." We each have a hot or cold button wherever we have accepted the idea that a person who has one characteristic *must* have certain others. These are some examples:

If she's Jewish, then she's good with money.

If he has long hair, he can't be a "solid citizen."

If he looks you in the eye, he can't be lying.

If she has young children, she'll want too much time off.

If he wears a three-piece suit, he can't be a good researcher.

If she's that feminine, she *can't* be an effective boss.

Sometimes each of these is true; sometimes they're false. But when you believe they're always true, you set yourself up to be manipulated:

He wears a business-like haircut and conservative suit—hoping you won't push too hard to find out how little auditing experience he's really had.

Her résumé emphasizes the college she graduated from and her membership in posh clubs—so you won't look closely at the number of jobs she's held in just three years.

And so it goes.

(**WHAT IF** you're really impressed with a candidate, but during the interview you suddenly push one of his cold buttons? What do you do then?)

Use Interviews Carefully

Interview, but don't put too much faith in the interview.

Marilyn Chan has always been systematic about things. Before she made her first selection as a supervisor, she read several books on interviewing. She wasn't surprised to find that researchers have been studying interviews for decades. But she was surprised to find out how unreliable interviews can be.

What Marilyn Chan discovered was something she really already knew: Candidates don't present honest, unvarnished pictures of themselves in interviews. They try to "sell" themselves and then try to "psyche out" the interviewer by saying exactly what he wants to hear.

Marilyn decided, like most managers, that she still wanted to interview the best-qualified candidates for her jobs. To get the most from her interviews, she decided she would use them to:

1. *Obtain information she couldn't easily get otherwise.* Does the candidate sound like he really understands the unit's work? What does he think it would be like to work in Marilyn's kind of workgroup?

2. *Observe behavior similar to that which the job requires.* If Marilyn is

looking for good people skills, she can judge how well the candidate handles the interview with her. If she needs someone good at communicating, she can evaluate how clearly the candidate explains things to her and how well he listens to what Marilyn says.

3. *Discover how the individual handled certain situations in the past.* What did he do when the computer went down on the night shift? How did he structure his personnel management course? Marilyn is very careful to ask what the person *did*, not what the person *would do.* She knows how easy it is to talk about a brilliant solution and how hard it is to really come up with one when you're on the spot.

EXAMPLE: Effective Interviewing

Marilyn is interviewing the three best candidates for her current vacancy. Each of them could do the job—she's fairly sure of that—but she's not sure which one would do it best.

She reads through their applications and tries to identify any missing information:

"Says he processed claims fully—did he authorize payment on his own signature?"

"She states that her degree is in business—what courses did she take?"

"I don't understand why he left that job in 1993—need to ask him."

Then Marilyn asks herself what she can learn in the interviews about their behavior. Most of her section's work is done over the phone, so how the candidates dress isn't significant. She decides to pay special attention to how they respond to her questions. Providing complete answers to client inquiries is an extremely important part of the job she's filling.

Finally, she makes a list of problem situations that each of the candidates may have encountered when dealing with clients. For example:

1. "Have you ever had to work with a very distrustful client? How did you handle the situation?"

2. "Please think of the last time you had a client who wouldn't let you go. What did you do?"

Now she's prepared to get as much information as possible from each interview.

(**WHAT IF** Marilyn wanted to know how well a candidate understood basic telephone courtesy? How could she find that out?)

Once she decided how to use the interviews, Marilyn set five goals for each interview. She would:

1. *Be completely prepared.* She had to know exactly what she wanted from the interview and how she planned to get it. If not, she might fail to get important information—and make a very poor impression on the interviewee.

2. *Give the interview her undivided attention.* Building a good rapport with the candidate is vital, and an interruption at the wrong time can be disastrous. Marilyn would do whatever she could to prevent interruptions: take her phone off the hook, close her door, even hang out a "Do Not Disturb" sign.

3. *Put the person at ease* first. Marilyn remembered all too well her own experience from the year before. The supervisor jumped right into the interview, and she'd stayed on edge the whole time. Most important, she was sure the supervisor had gotten a completely wrong impression of her. She was determined not to do this to someone else.

Marilyn asked herself how best to put someone at ease in the stressful atmosphere of an interview. Her answer: Start talking about something that is unrelated to the interview and interesting to the other person.

4. *Ask "open-ended" questions*—those that could not be answered with a simple "yes" or "no." Marilyn knew that this technique would draw the other person out more and wouldn't telegraph the answer she wanted.

5. *Listen at least 80 percent of the time.* Marilyn realized she couldn't learn much while she was doing the talking. She also suspected that some of the people she would be interviewing would try to keep *her* talking—so *they* wouldn't have to talk as much. They also could use what she said to help slant their own presentations.

EXAMPLE: Open-Ended Questions

These are some questions Marilyn might select (and some she would discard) for interviews:

"What do you like best about your current job?"

not

"Do you like to work with details?"

"What are you looking for in a boss?"

not

"Do you want a boss who lets you take the initiative?"

"Tell me about your typing."

not

"How fast can you type?"

"How do you feel about your progress in your career?"

not

"Are you satisfied with your progress in your career?"

(**WHAT IF** Marilyn wanted to find out if the candidate was truly interested in working for her organization? What kind of question(s) could she ask?)

Become Known as a Good Manager

The final key to good selecting is having the kind of reputation that makes good people want to work for you.

Let's go back to Henry Montoya again. He knows what he's looking for, and he works hard at selecting. He also has something else going for him—something even he doesn't fully realize.

Henry works hard at the kinds of skills this book describes. He develops successful workers. The rest of the organization recognizes that, and his people regularly get selected for promotion. As a result, people are anxious to work for Henry, and he always has top-flight workers applying to fill his jobs.

(Word gets around in an organization. When a manager becomes known as someone who treats people right, develops their skills, and helps them get ahead, good employees want to work for that manager. His selections get even better because now there is a better pool of applicants for each job.)

That's what has happened with Henry. People know that he develops successful workers, and they want to be part of his team. That makes his effective selecting practices even more effective, which results in better selections, who become very successful workers, who attract other good workers, . . .

In other words, nothing succeeds like success.

A QUICK SUMMARY

The managers described in this chapter know that effective selecting means finding individuals who have the right skills and the proper motivation, and who are good matches with their work and their workgroups.

They know that a candidate who doesn't pass all three tests of a good worker will take a great deal of extra supervisory time and effort to learn the job and stay with it. If they have to accept someone who doesn't meet all their standards, they'll select the candidate with good motivation who is less highly skilled over the one who has great skills but a problem attitude.

They know how to make effective selections. They:

1. Are realistic;
2. Gather lots of information about the candidates;
3. Are aware of their own hot (and cold) buttons;
4. Use interviews carefully to:
   a. Gather information they can't easily get otherwise,
   b. Observe behavior similar to that which the job requires, and
   c. Discover how the candidates handled certain situations in the past.

To be effective in interviews, managers know they must:

1. Be completely prepared,
2. Give the other person their undivided attention,

3. Put the other person at ease,
4. Ask open-ended questions, and
5. Listen at least 80 percent of the time.

They try to be the kind of manager who attracts high-quality candidates to their workgroups.

StretchMeter 3: SELECTING

1. I'm willing to take the time necessary to make good selections.

NEVER   0   1   2   3   4   5   6   7   8   **ALWAYS**

2. I know how to effectively gather information on candidates.

NEVER   0   1   2   3   4   5   6   7   8   **ALWAYS**

3. I can tell when someone pushes one of my hot buttons.

NEVER   0   1   2   3   4   5   6   7   8   **ALWAYS**

4. I know how to set goals for an interview.

NEVER   0   1   2   3   4   5   6   7   8   **ALWAYS**

5. I can keep the conversation on the subject I want to discuss.

NEVER   0   1   2   3   4   5   6   7   8   **ALWAYS**

6. I can give the other person my complete attention.

NEVER   0   1   2   3   4   5   6   7   8   **ALWAYS**

7. I know how to put the other person at ease quickly.

NEVER   0   1   2   3   4   5   6   7   8   **ALWAYS**

8. I ask open-ended questions.

NEVER   0   1   2   3   4   5   6   7   8   **ALWAYS**

9. I'm able to listen at least 80 percent of the time.

NEVER   0   1   2   3   4   5   6   7   8   **ALWAYS**

Selecting ASAP

1. If you haven't been willing to take the time you need to make good selections, you may still have the idea that what's important is the "work" that you do. You need to remember that selecting is one of the seven critical activities of Phase One Management. If you keep that clearly in mind, you'll soon be taking the time you need.

2. Effectively gathering information can be difficult, but it's absolutely essential. This tip will help you do it: Pick out your two or three best workers and your two or three poorest (if you have any). Get their personnel files. Go through their employment information and see if you could have predicted what kind of workers they would be from the records. (Even if you can't, you should have a clearer idea of what to look for in the future.)

3. It's not very difficult to tell when a hot (or cold) button has been pushed: When you have a strong positive or negative reaction to someone or something based on one or a few of his or its characteristics, a button has been pushed. Use a Reaction Alert like the one described in the ASAP for Chapter 1 to keep track of how many times this happens in, say, a week. When you start paying attention in this way, you'll start to see patterns in your reactions. The clearer the patterns become, the easier it will be to protect yourself against them.

4. You must have well-thought-out, realistic goals for an interview if you want it to be successful. For practice, prepare to interview three candidates for a vacancy. If you have a real vacancy, great. If not, imagine that you're interviewing three workers—in your own or another workgroup—that you know only slightly. Write down what you want to know about each candidate when the interview is over. Then write down what you know about each candidate *now*. The difference between the two lists for each candidate is your goal for that interview.

5. Keeping a conversation on the subject you want to discuss is an easy skill to work on (though not necessarily an easy one to master). Starting tomorrow morning, have a minimum of two conversations per day for a week in which you hold the conversation to a specific topic for at least five minutes. The more

subtly and naturally you can do this, the better. (Hint: One of the best ways to keep a conversation focused where you want it is to keep asking relevant questions.)

6. Paying complete attention to a person you're talking with is a skill that is valuable in many different situations. Copy the pattern in ASAP 5: For a week, have a minimum of two conversations a day in which you concentrate completely on the other person for at least five minutes. If you rated yourself low in ASAP 5 also, you can combine the two in the same conversations.

7. It would be a shame to do everything else right and then have the interview fail because the person you were interviewing couldn't loosen up. Within the next week, create a list of at least ten conversation topics that could be used to break the ice. One method is to listen to the other people talking and to write down some of the topics they discuss in a relaxed and enthusiastic way. Test your list be talking about a topic with others—preferably people you've just met. Replace any of the topics that don't work well. Now you have a list of topics to use to open interviews.

8. Asking effective, open-ended questions is one of the most useful skills you can have. For the next week, carry your counter with you. Count each time you ask a question that can be answered with a "yes" or a "no." By how much can you reduce your daily count in a week? The second week, count each open-ended question you ask. By how much can you increase this total?

9. Being a good listener is another valuable skill (and one that will be discussed again in this book). For the next week, pick at least one conversation a day in which you will listen no less than 80 percent of the time. Do it. If possible, have someone who knows what you're trying to do listen to the conversation—then ask him if you actually listened as much as you thought you did. Typically, each of us believes that we listen more than an outside observer believes we do. If that's the case with you, change it.

CHAPTER 6

Guiding

PHASE ONE MANAGEMENT	
Structuring	C
Selecting	O
	M
Guiding	M
	U
Correcting	N
	I
Motivating	C
	A
Delegating	T
	I
Supporting	N
	G

In this chapter, you'll find useful information on:

Seeing that workers know *what to do.*

Making sure that they know *how to do it well.*

Ensuring that workers understand the importance of quality.

Paying special attention to workers who have just made major transitions.

This chapter will provide you with the tools you need to begin developing workers who know what to do *and* how to do it well.

WHAT IS EFFECTIVE GUIDING?

L ee Chen learned the hard way how important effective guiding is. When he first came to America, he spoke almost no English. He'll never forget how difficult it was to adapt to a new culture, get a job, and learn to speak English, all at the same time. Lee remembers the people who were patient with him while he was learning, and those who weren't.

Now Lee is a manager. Most of the people he selects already speak English and most of them know something about the work of the section. But Lee still concentrates on guiding them carefully until they learn everything they need to know to be successful workers.

One of Lee's top priorities is making sure that each new worker knows *what to do*. He carefully outlines what the section does and explains each of the deadlines that must be met. Then he explains why each job is necessary. After a week or two, Lee sends each new worker to visit the section that uses the reports he creates, and has the manager of that section explain the purpose of those reports.

Next, Lee concentrates on seeing that each new employee knows *how to do his job well*. Lee assigns the person to one of his senior employees who knows how to get the job done efficiently and well. During the training, Lee talks frequently with the trainers, making sure that they're patient and encouraging with new workers.

There's one point that Lee repeats over and over to each new worker: "We have to do high-quality work. I want you to learn to work with great efficiency, and I want you to perform tasks on time—*but* I want you to do them right the first time. We are too busy to spend time doing work over again."

WHY IS EFFECTIVE GUIDING IMPORTANT?

Ask Julia Szabo, she'll tell you:

> "When I started in this job, I thought it was best to allow people to pick things up on their own. It lets them show initiative," I said. "Boy, was I wrong! They may have had initiative, but it took forever for them to learn to do things properly.

> "That's when I changed my tactics. Now I let my best people train the new ones because they enjoy doing it. But I check to make sure that the new workers are learning what I want them to learn. I also work with the new people, just to reassure myself.

My new system works; the new workers learn the job faster, and they do it better.

"I also found it was a good way for all of us to get to know the new person. Working with him conveys the feeling that we all care about his performance. And we get a better sense of what the person is like and what we need to emphasize in his training.

"Something else is important. It's easy to fall into the habit of paying attention to people only when they foul up, which is a negative way of managing. Putting some time and energy into guiding your workgroup turns this around. I get used to helping them, and my people start to see me more as a coach than a boss. It's easier now for me to correct them, and they're more honest with me when they have a problem.

"There's one other thing I should mention. Most of the people in my section started in this department right after college. A couple of years ago, though, we began promoting some clerks from other departments. At first it didn't look like things were going to work out—and then I suddenly realized what the problem was. The new people didn't understand how what we do is different from what clerks do. They were trying to do our job, but they were looking at it as a clerical job.

"As soon as I understood, I began working with them to show them how the jobs differed. One of them just couldn't get it, but the others have turned out to be excellent workers. I think the moral of this is that when a job represents a big change for someone, you must take extra care to see that he's guided properly."

HOW DO I GUIDE EFFECTIVELY?

Harold Taplinger is a graduate student in business school. As part of a course assignment, he's talking with Lee and Julia about how they became so effective at guiding their employees. The following is part of their conversation:

Guiding New Workers

Harold: Do both of you use senior workers to train new workers?
Lee: I introduce the new person to everyone in the unit and talk about

what we do and why it is done. Then I turn him over to my senior workers for training. I keep up with the person's progress, though, and I guide him myself on the things I think are most important.

Julia: That's what I had been doing, too. We're trying something a little different now. I sent my two top people to an on-the-job-training course, and they're going to be our official "tutors" for the new people. We've prepared a training manual that outlines what a new worker needs to know, and the tutors will use it. I will stay involved enough to get to know each person and establish a coaching relationship with him.

Harold: Have you tried out your "tutoring" system yet?

Julia: We're right in the middle of our first trial now. I'm not certain yet, but it looks like it's working well.

Lee: I have thought of trying Julia's way, but the members of my group get such pleasure from working with new people that they all want to take part and help. They like to work as a team, and I have been afraid to do anything that might interfere with that.

EXAMPLE: Guiding New Workers

Bilal has just come to work for Julia. She sets aside an hour at the beginning of Bilal's first day to talk with him and find what he needs to learn to do his new job successfully.

She already knows from his application that he's done the same work for two other organizations. During their conversation, she learns that his skills are well developed but that the other organizations' procedures were very different. She decides that he needs to learn her workgroup's procedures first.

Fortunately, the workgroup has several jobs needing analysis that are good training material for Bilal. Julia calls in Winston, one of her most experienced workers. She explains to him that she wants Bilal to analyze the jobs, with Winston to help him. She makes it clear that Bilal has the skills and that Winston's job is to show him the procedures he should use.

Julia asks Winston to start by helping Bilal identify which factors should be used in analyzing the first two jobs. Then she asks them both to get back to her so that Bilal can explain why he selected those factors. This will give her a clearer idea of how much training Bilal will need, and it will also help her get to know him a little better.

(**WHAT IF** Bilal lacks several important skills? How should Julia start him out?)

Sharing Skills

Lee: Let me tell you about something I have begun with my experienced workers. For a long time, I had believed that some of them were just naturally better workers than others. Then I watched one of my very good workers help another one, and that one really improved. It started me thinking, and then I began asking workers with a recognized skill to demonstrate it for the others. It is having some good results.

Julia: What about the ones you don't ask to demonstrate? Don't they get put out?

Lee: I have been lucky because I have been able to find something for each person to talk about. Even our newest worker developed something that the others had not discovered. They all have tremendous enthusiasm now for helping each other.

Julia: I've also noticed how some workers like to pass on their skills. Now that my people all know each other well, some of the best workers voluntarily help others with difficult jobs. In fact, I've just appointed someone in the group who isn't a tutor to be the official "helper." She was very pleased and suggested several skills she thought she could share with others.

Harold: Some teachers say that everyone can be taught to do a job as well as the best person. It sounds like you'd agree.

Lee: I do not know if it applies to everyone, but I have seen workers improve greatly by learning from others.

Julia: I have, too. I believe that most people really want to do a good job, and I think it's important to be patient with them and encourage them to help each other. That's one reason why I like the word "guide." I'd rather think of myself as a guide than a "boss" or a "know-it-all."

Harold: Yes, but don't you have to "chew-out" workers, too?

Lee: I do not find that necessary very often. Besides, I believe that topic will be covered in the next chapter.

EXAMPLE: Sharing Skills

At first, Lee wants his most skilled workers to start sharing their best skills with the others right away. As he thinks more about it, though, he realizes there are potential problems. His workgroup hasn't worked together long enough to completely trust each other. He's afraid that those who need to develop their skills might feel insulted by the demonstrations.

So, Lee waits for a while. He arranges things so that different workers get the opportunity to work closely with each other, which builds up the trust he needs. It also gives the workers a chance to see just how skilled some of the others are. In fact, he notices several times that one of them will ask another to share a specific skill.

Several months pass. Then Lee gets his chance during a group meeting, when Amy thanks John for showing her a particularly good shortcut.

"I think each of us has something to share with the others," Lee says. "I would like to have a meeting every other Friday and turn the meeting over to a different person each time. I want that person to select what he feels is his best skill and explain it to the others. How do you feel about that?"

A few workers hesitate, but most of them are willing to try it. Lee sets the first meeting up with Rafael leading it. Because Rafael is well known as the most skilled worker in the group, Lee thinks no one will be embarrassed to learn from him.

They aren't, and the session goes very well. After that, everyone is enthusiastic about the idea.

(**WHAT IF** Lee wanted to start the program, but no one gave him an opening? How could he have initiated it in that situation?)

The Importance of Quality

Julia: Can I change the subject a little? We haven't talked at all about quality, and I think quality is very important.

Harold: My professors are saying that American companies must continue to improve their quality if we're to continue being competitive internationally.

Julia: I don't know about internationally, but I know that my people *want* to produce high quality. I think most workers do. When I started with a manufacturing outfit across town years ago, we didn't have much competition, and what we built was pretty sloppy. And the people who worked there hated that! I've never been anywhere that the morale was so low, and the poor work they put out was the primary cause.

Lee: I know. When I became a first-level manager, nearly a third of the workers in my section were spending most of their time reviewing the others' work. What they meant by "reviewing" was inspecting. We have changed that, and now everybody feels better. And we have increased the work we do and the quality of it. Inspecting is a very inefficient way to get quality work.

Julia: Yes. I think my people get tired of hearing me say, "Do it right the first time," but I keep on saying it. I want them to *expect* to get it right without anyone else having to look at it.

Harold: Some books call that "conformance to requirements."

Lee: I believe it is better to speak of conforming to what people who use our products expect. These are really our "customers," and we need to produce what they want. Once every three months, I take several of my people and we meet with some workers from the unit that uses what we produce. We want to make sure that we are giving them what they desire and that we are giving it to them the first time.

Julia: Yes, I do the same thing, but not on a regular schedule. We've made quite a few changes because of what our "customers" have told us. I emphasize the importance of doing quality work to my people. I'm also going to do something else I think is exciting. Marketing has agreed to let three of my people sit in on its next focus group so that they can see what customers do with the information we research.

EXAMPLE: Improving Quality

Paul finds that he has a quality problem on the day he takes over the Routine Claims Section.

This section receives each routine health insurance claim and decides what payment should be made. After a claims clerk has made the decision, the claim moves to the Claims Payment Section next door. There, an authorization clerk reviews the decision before payment is made.

When Paul looks at the statistics for the previous week, he's shocked. Fifteen percent of the decisions made by the claims clerks were turned back by the authorization clerks and had to be redone.

Paul talks informally with the claims clerks about the situation. He finds that they:

1. Resent having the authorization clerks check their work,

2. Often don't worry about doing sloppy work because they know it will be caught and they can redo it, and

3. Feel that the authorization clerks "ought to have to work hard because they get paid more than we do."

Paul realizes that the current situation is wasting a great deal of time and effort and making everyone angry in the process. In the long run, he plans to work with the supervisor of the Payment Section to develop cooperation between the two units. But he wants to produce some improvement right away.

Paul would like to post each clerk's error rate but is afraid that will just make them angrier. In talking to the clerks, he finds that most of them want to be promoted to the Nonroutine Claims Section—but that their section's reputation keeps most of them from even being considered for openings there.

Paul has found what he's looking for. He persuades the Nonroutine Claims Section supervisor to give a two-hour training session on processing difficult claims every other Friday afternoon. Then he sets the policy that any clerk who holds his error rate down to five percent or less for two weeks can attend the training session.

It starts slowly, but before too long, every clerk's error rate is under five percent. The clerks are enthusiastic about the training sessions, but something more important happens: They begin to feel better about themselves and their work—and the Payment Section begins to feel better about them.

There's even another benefit: Because the clerks feel better about their work, they aren't as defensive when Paul makes suggestions for improving it.

(**WHAT IF** Paul's next step is to reduce the error rate to two percent or less? How could he do it?)

Guiding Workers in Transition

Julia: Harold, there's one other thing we need to talk about—managing workers who're making major transitions.

Harold: I'm not quite sure what you mean by "major transitions."

Julia: Well, most people who come into my jobs are pretty well prepared for them. We have to teach them the specifics of the jobs, but they learn them quickly. This isn't always true, though. We've promoted a number of clerks in the last few years, and it has been a big transition for them to move from clerical to analytical work.

Harold: Do you mean they weren't able to do it?

Julia: No—once they understood the difference, they learned very well. But my experienced workers and I had to spend a lot of time making the difference clear to them.

Lee: It is not just clerks. When I became a first-level manager, no one explained to me what a big change that was. I kept trying to do the work along with my people. We got into a very large mess before I learned that my job was now something very different.

Julia: I had that problem, too. And there are many other situations where people have to make big jumps. It's tough for someone who is on his first job or for someone coming back to work after raising a family.

Lee: Yes, and it is very hard to go from a job out in the plant to one in the offices here. I can also tell you that it is difficult when you feel like an outsider. In my case, that was language and not knowing American culture, but it can be many things.

Julia: I know. I was the first female manager here, and I felt like an outsider for quite a while.

Harold: Let me make sure I understand this—because it's new to me. You're saying that you have to be particularly careful when you're guiding workers who've made a major career move. These are people who've moved into very different kinds of work, or who're working for the first time or returning to work after several years off. Also, people from different ethnic groups or backgrounds, who may feel strange in the workgroup, need extra attention. Is that right?

Julia (nodding): That's it.

EXAMPLE: Transitional Workers

Arlene is the first clerk to be promoted to job analyst in Julia's branch. She started as a records clerk and then worked her way up to senior clerk in the training section. Because she's very intelligent and gets along extremely well with other people, Julia selected her as a trainee analyst.

Although Arlene tries hard, she just isn't catching on to the work. Several of the other analysts complain to Julia that they have to explain things over and over to her, and even then, she often doesn't understand. Everybody likes her, but they are running out of patience.

Julia makes it a point to work with Arlene herself. She finds that Arlene keeps asking questions instead of using her own judgment. She mentions this to Arlene once; the woman gets flustered and upset, and Julia has to break off the discussion.

Julia doesn't want to give up on Arlene because she remembers how hard it was when she became the first female in the division. One day, as she's driving home from work, she suddenly realizes what the problem is.

Julia talks with Arlene the next day and confirms her thought. Arlene was working in a job where her function was to apply rules. Arlene's greatest skill, in fact, is that she can identify and apply very complicated rules. But they're still rules. She has no experience at analyzing a situation—which is a very different mental skill.

Julia starts to work with Arlene on basic analytic skills and sends her to a few courses. The going is slow at first, but then Arlene begins to understand the difference. . . .

Two years later, Arlene is the worker assigned to train the new analyst who's just been promoted from a clerical position in the recruiting branch.

(**WHAT IF** Arlene had been an analyst before but had been out of the job market for 15 years to raise a family? What kind of transitional help would she have been most apt to need?)

Harold: Thank you. I think I can write up the heart of what you've
said as . . .

A QUICK SUMMARY

1. It's very important to help new people become a part of the
   workgroup.
2. New workers must know what to do and how to do it well.
3. Doing it well means doing quality work the first time.
4. Managers need to be certain that new workers are learning the right
   things, whether the managers are teaching the new people themselves or have assigned that responsibility to senior workers.
5. Anyone who trains a new worker should think of himself as a guide
   or coach, not a boss or a judge.
6. Managers especially need to pay close attention to people who are
   making major transition and provide them with the extra guidance they need.

StretchMeter 4: GUIDING

1. My workers want to do a good job.

NEVER   1   2   3   4   5   6   7   8   ALWAYS

2. I help others learn insted of doing the job myself.

NEVER   1   2   3   4   5   6   7   8   ALWAYS

3. My workers know what our customers[1] want.

NEVER   1   2   3   4   5   6   7   8   ALWAYS

4. My workers know how to do all their tasks well.

NEVER   1   2   3   4   5   6   7   8   ALWAYS

5. My workers produce high quality work.

NEVER   1   2   3   4   5   6   7   8   ALWAYS

6. I am a coach instead of a boss.[2]

NEVER   1   2   3   4   5   6   7   8   ALWAYS

7. I know which of my workers are making major transitions.

NEVER   1   2   3   4   5   6   7   8   ALWAYS

8. I give special attention to workers making major transitions.

NEVER   1   2   3   4   5   6   7   8   ALWAYS

---

[1]Remember, your customers are those who use whatever you produce. For many workgroups, that's another part of the organization, not the final customer.

[2]This book keeps referring to being a boss as something you want to avoid, but it keeps referring to your "boss"—not your "manager" or your "coach." Here's why: If you have an understanding and helpful manager, that's great. If you don't, though, you can't wait for him to change so that you can succeed. He may be a "boss" in all of the worst senses of the word, but he's still your boss. He may change, but he hasn't. If you're going to succeed, you're going to do it working for him just as he is now.

Guiding ASAP

1. If you don't believe that your workers want to do a good job most of the time, you're not going to give them proper guidance. Choose a worker you feel certain isn't particularly interested in doing a good job. Think about the last three mistakes he made. Now, how could those mistakes have been caused by not knowing how to do something rather than not wanting to do it? Don't quit until you have an answer to that question (even if you don't believe it's true). For the next week, act as though you think that "not knowing" is the answer. What happens?

2. Doing things yourself instead of helping others learn to do them is a bad habit—one that calls for a Reaction Alert. (Don't know what that is? See the ASAP for Chapter 1.) Use your Reaction Alert to train yourself to help others learn, as a substitute for your habitual reaction of doing things yourself.[3]

3. To paraphrase an old saying, if your workers don't know what your customers want, it's going to be hard to tell when they've given it to them. Make an appointment now to have someone from the section that uses what you produce come and talk with your group about how that section uses your output. If you have more than one customer, make plans to have each of them come in and do this—or for your workgroup to visit their areas and see for themselves how your product is used.

4. If your workers don't know how to do all their tasks well, you're wasting their talents. Your first step is to determine what doing a task "well" means. Pick one task—an important one—and locate the worker who does it best. Observe how he does it. Then see that the other workers learn how to do the task that way. Keep it up until everyone knows how to do everything well. (Afraid this will take months? Okay, let it take months.)

5. If your workers don't produce high quality work, you have dissatisfied workers—no matter how good everything else is.

[3]I know that Reaction Alerts work for this, because that's what I developed the one on my desk for. Specifically, I wanted to break myself of the bad habit of solving problems for my workers. Because I want them to be successful, I want them to be good at problem solving. My Reaction Alert reminds me not to take their problems away from them and solve them, but to help them understand and solve them themselves.

You can't change the situation overnight with pep talks or by publishing a new policy. But you can pick one process or output that can be measured—today—and start measuring it. When you reduce errors to zero, go on to the next one. WARNING: This is a never-ending process. (Pick an important process or output if you can, but pick one—and begin to improve it.)

6. A boss gets results by *forcing* his workers to do their jobs. A coach gets results by *helping* his workers do their jobs. A successful manager is more coach than boss. If you're spending too much time being a boss, you may believe that your workers don't really *want* to do a good job. Try the exercise in ASAP 1 with the worker you have to boss the most.

7. Even very bright, very motivated workers can have difficulties when they're making a major transition from one job to another (or from not working to working). Identify someone in your group who is making a major transition and find out how he thinks and feels about it. When you've made yourself aware of the problems he faces, find out tactfully if there are others making a similar transition. (If none of your workers is in transition, see if you can find someone in another workgroup who is, and talk with him to get a better feel for the problems workers encounter in that situation.)

8. It doesn't help to know who's making a major transition if you don't do anything about it. Try the direct approach. Sit down with each person who's making a significant transition and ask him to list the problems as he sees them. Listen carefully, because you may have to hear some of it "between the lines." Once you know what each person's situation is, you can guide him more effectively toward becoming a successful worker.

CHAPTER 7

Correcting

PHASE ONE MANAGEMENT	
Structuring	C
Selecting	O M
Guiding	M U
Correcting	N I
Motivating	C A
Delegating	T I
Supporting	N G

In this chapter, you'll find useful information on:

How important effective feedback is for successful performance, especially for new workers.

An effective strategy to use when correcting workers.

The benefits of a system that gives prompt performance feedback directly to workers.

This information will aid you in further developing workers who know what to do and how to do it. It will also assist you in finding ways to ensure that workers know when they've done their jobs well. In turn, this will help your workers become motivated to want to do well.

WHAT IS EFFECTIVE CORRECTING?

Raymond Hill had always thought that the way to improve work-ers' performance was to tell people when they weren't doing a good job.

If his workgroup's reject rate got too high, Ray would call together those workers who had made mistakes and tell them that he expected them to do better. If the reject rate was particularly bad that week, he made sure that he really chewed on them. When that didn't work, he tried appealing to their pride—without any better results. Ray was on the verge of quitting as a manager when his organization sent him to a "refresher" course in management.

"I didn't think what the instructors were saying in the course would work on the job," Ray admits, "but things were so bad I was willing to try anything. I was amazed at what happened. I didn't believe it at first, but I sure believe it now.

"The first thing I found out was that a lot of my people didn't even know when they were doing things wrong. The pieces they pro-duced went on to the next section, and if those pieces weren't right, they'd be fixed by the workers there and marked down on the reject summary that was sent to me each week. The people in my group who made the mistakes usually didn't know they were making them. They didn't even know I was talking to *them* when I yelled about the rejects.

"Then I found that my two best workers were doing something about this situation on their own. Whenever I really yelled about a bad prod-uct, they'd go over to the next section and ask a worker there to show them what was wrong. If it was something they had been fouling up, they'd change it. That way, they stayed out of trouble, but no one else in the group knew their secret.

"Well, to make a long story short, I made a lot of changes. What they really amounted to is this:

1. I make sure that every worker knows how *he* is doing. I still get the overall reject figure, but I make sure I have a breakdown for each individual, too.

2. When someone is making a mistake, I see that he knows about it right away. If I wait a week, that worker may produce bad products for a week. So, I get the data every evening, and the next morning I discuss any problems with the workers involved.

3. If workers are not producing good products, they also need to

know what they have to change to improve. That may sound silly, but I found that most of my people who didn't seem to care actually didn't know what they'd done wrong, or why it was wrong, or how to do better.

"As a matter of fact, over the past six years I've had only one worker who didn't produce a good product once he knew what he'd done wrong, why it was wrong, and how to do it right."

WHY IS EFFECTIVE CORRECTING IMPORTANT?

Ellie Donahue has been a supervisor for just two years. Before she began this job, she read a book on successful management that emphasized effective correcting. She tried doing what the book suggested, and it worked.

Ellie discovered that quick correction is very important with new workers. If this doesn't happen, they'll learn how to do their jobs incorrectly. New workers need to know when they're doing their jobs *correctly*, too—so they can keep performing that way.

Ellie learned that experienced workers may need correction just as much as new ones. When things just go along and nobody says anything, workers sometimes fall into bad habits and produce sloppy work. She wants to avoid having any of her good workers ruined this way. Ellie's found that when each worker in her group knows how he's doing and knows what Ellie expects from him, this doesn't happen.

HOW DO I CORRECT EFFECTIVELY?

Correcting Is Okay

First of all, as either Ray or Ellie will tell you, correcting is okay—as long as you understand it and use it effectively. It's easy to think of correcting as something negative, such as pointing out to someone that he's wrong. And many people have painful memories of being harshly "corrected" by their parents and teachers.

"That's not what I mean by 'correcting,' at all," Ellie says. "I try to be very tactful, and I don't correct anyone in front of others. The most important point, though, is that I believe that my workers *want* to do things right. I'm not trying to 'shape them up'; I'm giving them the information they need to do the job the way they want to do it. That's a completely different thing."

Ray continues the theme: "Exactly. A worker who makes a mistake can't correct the mistake until he knows what, why, and how: *What* he did wrong, *why* it was wrong, and *how* to do it right.

"If you give an individual that information and he continues to make mistakes, you may have a problem employee. But when the worker doesn't have this information, the manager is the problem."

"We certainly agree on that," Ellie adds. "And the worker needs all three pieces of information:

1. When mistakes are made, your worker has to know w*hat* he didn't do correctly (or well). Without this input, he'll either continue to think the work is acceptable or may completely misunderstand what was wrong.

2. Your worker has to understand w*hy* it was wrong. People don't usually make mistakes because they lack intelligence. They may leave a step out or may do the steps in the wrong order. They may try to reason out how it ought to be done—but don't know enough to reason correctly. Unless they find out what they did was wrong, they can't know just what needs to be done to correct it.

3. Finally, your worker has to know ho*w* to do the job right, which is different from you telling him to do it right. He learns how when you *tell* him what to do, *show* him how to do it, and then watch him *practice* doing it.

"The point is that I think most errors are made because workers don't have enough information to prevent them. Our first responsibility as managers is to see that this doesn't happen with *our* workers."

EXAMPLE: Effective Correcting, I

"Ray, I just don't know about Evelyn Jones," Howard said, frowning. "I don't think she's ever going to learn how to set up a jig correctly. I've showed her how three times," explained Tony. "And I just had to set it up for her again."

"Hmmm. Does she know that she made a mistake?" Ray Hill asked.

"Sure—I told her."

"Do you know what her mistake was?"

"No—and I don't see what that has to do with it. I showed her how to do it correctly, and I told her when she did it wrong. That ought to be enough! She should have more common sense."

"No, Howard, what you've done isn't enough—and it has nothing to do with common sense. If I'd trained you that way when you first came to work here, I'd still be setting up jigs for *you*. Let's go over there, and I'll show you what I mean."

"Evelyn, Howard tells me you're having a problem setting up your jig when you change runs."

"Yes, Mr. Hill, I am. I don't understand it—I know I'm doing everything Howard tells me to do."

"How about taking it apart and letting me watch you put it back together, okay?" Evelyn nodded. She hesitated a moment, then disassembled the jig and began reassembling it.

"That's it," Ray said. "You're trying to anchor the back before the front of it is set, which prevents the tongue from seating properly. Howard, show her what I mean."

Howard lifted the jig slightly and pointed to the problem. "Oh, I see it now," Evelyn said excitedly.

"Now, Howard, show her how it should be done." He did. "Okay, take it apart again. Evelyn, why don't you try it?" She did, and smiled as parts slid smoothly together.

"Thanks," she said.

"Evelyn, I was just telling Howard how important it is for someone who makes an error to know what the error is, why it is an error, and how to correct it. Howard, are you a believer now?"

Howard grinned sheepishly and nodded.

(**WHAT IF** Ray had just told Evelyn she'd get it if she'd only pay more attention? What do you think would have happened?)

Correcting a Worker

Ellie frowned thoughtfully. "There's another aspect to correcting: It's not always clear whether the worker made a mistake or not. For instance, my group primarily does quick-and-dirty custom work. I don't mean we do sloppy work—we don't. But a lot of what we do is writing short data analysis utilities for some special purpose. A researcher will call us and say he needs to do such-and-such an analysis. One of my programmers will knock something out, give it a quick test, and send it up.

"The problem is that we don't always furnish what the person wanted. Then he complains, and I have to get involved. Before I talk to my programmer, though, I don't know whether the programmer made an error or our customer was unclear about what was needed."

"I see what you're saying," Ray commented. "Most of the time, it's obvious if one of my people makes an error. I get together with him; use the what, why, and how method; and correct the error. But with your group, you have to determine first whether your programmer goofed or your customer failed to describe what he wanted well enough. I can see how that complicates matters."

"It does. When I first took over the section, I really wanted to please our customers. When a customer complained, I leaned on my people. That didn't work very well. The people in my group felt I wasn't supporting them and wasn't interested in their side of the story."

"What did you do?"

"Well, I've worked out a way of correcting that succeeds most of the time. It goes like this: First of all, when I discuss performance with a worker, it's no one else's business. I ask him to join me somewhere where we can talk privately. I'm sure you do that."

Ray nodded emphatically.

"Next, I don't assume that I know what happened. I want to listen to my worker, and I want him to know that I'm willing to listen. That means I spend the time necessary to find out how my worker sees the situation. Sometimes I hear what I expect to hear. Sometimes, though, I find I've gotten the wrong idea—it's important that I get corrected, too.

"My goal is for us to discuss the situation until we both see it the same way. It doesn't always happen, but I know that when it does, it makes things a lot easier for us both."

"What if you don't think your worker did anything wrong—what do you do then?" Ray asked.

"That's easy. If I'm satisfied he did a good job, I make sure he knows I'm satisfied. Then I thank him for discussing it with me, and the talk ends there. If I'm not satisfied, if the worker really didn't do what should have been done, I try to let him realize this for himself. If he does, I know we'll be able to correct the problem quickly. When the worker takes responsibility for the problem, I can put all my energy into helping him find a solution.

"You know as well as I do that the worker doesn't always recognize his error, which means that I have to point it out. I do it as objectively as I can; I never make it sound like I've caught him at something or I'm blaming him for something. Unless the worker proves otherwise to me, I figure that he's just as interested in doing a good job as I am in having it done.

"Finally, I make sure that the worker understands exactly what he did wrong, why it was wrong, and how to do it right. If necessary, I go through the tell–show–practice sequence again. I know that different people learn at different speeds, and I don't mind repeating guidance I've already given."

EXAMPLE: Effective Correcting, II

"Jared, I want to talk to you about the data conversion program you did for Dr. Stennis," Ellie began. "She says it gives her the wrong answer about a third of the time."

"Yes, I guess it does. She's using negative fractions, and the conversion routine wasn't designed to handle them. If she'd told me everything she wanted when she first called, this wouldn't have happened."

"What did she say she wanted?"

"She called down in a hurry, like she always does, and said she needed a data converter. I figured she was working with the same kind of problems as Dr. Yankelovich, so I took the converter I did for him and doctored it a little bit."

"You didn't ask her for any details about the data?"

"No, that shouldn't be my job. She's the Ph.D.—she ought to be able to tell me what she wants."

"Maybe so—but wouldn't everybody have been better off if you'd asked her a few questions? I know you're not happy that she thinks you made a mistake."

"No, I'm not. And in answer to your question, it gripes me; but, yes, I should have asked her. The fact that she didn't tell me what she wanted is no excuse for me to turn out something she thinks is wrong. I have more pride than that."

"I know you do. Now let me make sure we both understand. You didn't give her the right kind of converter because you didn't take the time to ask the right questions. Next time, you're going to find out what you need to know—even if you have to drag it out of them."

Jared grinned. "Yep—even if I have to drag it out of them."

(**WHAT IF** Ellie had begun by assuming that Jared had fouled up the data conversion program? How do you think Jared would have responded?)

"That's good," Ray said. "Let me add one point to it. There are really three different reasons why a worker can make a mistake. He:

1. May not know how to do the job correctly,
2. May know, but does it carelessly, or
3. May do it wrong willfully—either intending to do it wrong or not caring whether it's wrong or not.

"When you're correcting a worker, it's important first to find out whether the employee's mistake was willful or careless or the result of not knowing what to do. One of the worst mistakes a manager can make is to treat someone who wasn't sure what to do as though he deliberately did something wrong."

"I certainly agree with that," Ellie replied. "In fact, I find that most errors are made because people don't know what to do. They may never have been told or they may have forgotten, or they haven't taken the time to think it through."

"Right," Ray nodded. "When I find a worker who's made a mistake, I assume that it was an honest mistake. If it was, and I give the person the guidance needed to correct it, I won't see the mistake again.

"On the other hand, if the same mistake pops up again, I start to wonder. Then the individual has to persuade me that it wasn't carelessness or lack of attention or just indifference. In other words, I assume that most conscientious workers won't make the same mistake twice."

Prompt, Automatic Feedback

Bobby Joe Fritz, a first-level manager from the next department, comes up just then. "Do you know what I've been trying to do? I've been trying to set up a system so that my workers find out for themselves how they're doing. I figure that if they don't have to get it through me, it can't turn into an argument.

"I've worked something out with the unit that uses our output. If one of my workers produces a document that has an error, the person who uses the document calls the worker directly. My worker either corrects the error over the phone or picks up the document immediately, redoes it, and returns it.

"I had a little trouble persuading both my workgroup and the other unit to adopt this plan, but they finally agreed to test it for 90 days. Our output has improved so much since we started it, though, that I don't think anyone will want to quit using it when the test period is over."

"That's very interesting," Ellie said. "Your people really like it?"

"Most of them do. They know that if they make an error, they'll find out about it quickly. They also know that they won't get blamed for someone else's errors—and that's important. Mike Samuels is the exception; he didn't like it when *I* told him he'd made an error, and he doesn't like it when *someone else* tells him, either. The others think it's great—particularly because I don't even know about an error unless it's repeated. As a matter of fact, the other section doesn't inform me of an error unless it's repeated three times within a two-week period."

"But how do you know how well your people are doing overall?" Ray asked.

"Oh, I still get the biweekly report. It gives me summary figures that tell me how the group is doing as a whole. It's great for making sure we stay within our targets, and I always post it for everyone to see. But I never try to use it to correct individual workers."

The Worker's Responsibility

"What about conduct?" Ray asked. "We've been talking about correcting *performance*, and that's most of what we do. But what about the conduct problems we run into?"

Ellie responded, "I look at conduct almost the same way I do performance. I make sure that everyone knows all the rules, and I try to keep the rules as simple and as few as I can—you know, common sense. After that, each of my people is responsible for his own performance and conduct. I'm not anyone's den mother or schoolteacher, —I should not go around taking responsibility for how he behaves."

"I agree," Bobby Joe said. "This Mike Samuels I mentioned before is a good example of a conduct problem. I've talked with him several times, and I've run out of talk. I've made clear what we expect from him and that I won't tolerate anything else. He knows that the next time he's rude to someone in another department, he's in deep trouble. I feel like you do, Ellie—it's his responsibility to improve. The ball's in his court."

EXAMPLE: Dealing with Continued Poor Conduct

Bobby Joe had already talked to Mike several times. Mike knew exactly:

What he was doing wrong (being rude to the people who pointed out his errors),

Why it was wrong (he was insulting people who were trying to help him perform well and was refusing to accept useful feedback), and

How to correct it (accept the feedback constructively).

In this final conversation, Bobby Joe gave Mike one last chance to explain himself as they sat together in Bobby Joe's office:

"They keep picking on me. No one else in the unit gets called anywhere near as many times as I do."

"Do you think that's because no one else makes as many errors?"

"It doesn't matter. It's insulting, and I don't like it."

"Okay, Mike, I understand how you feel about it. Now I want to make sure you understand my situation: First of all, our prompt feedback system is policy, and I expect everyone to follow it. Second, rudeness is never acceptable. I don't care what the reason for it is; it simply isn't acceptable.

"Mike, you have a choice. You can clean up your act, do what your job requires, and everything will be fine. If you're not willing to do that, you'd probably better look for another job because I won't tolerate your rudeness another time.

"I've done my part. You know the rules, and you know the consequences if you don't follow them. Mike, we really would like to see you shape up. The people here like you. But we can't make the choice for you. . . . "

(**WHAT IF** the first thing Mike had said was "I've been trying to be nice to those people, but they keep accusing me of making mistakes that I'm not making?" What should Bobby Joe have done then?)

"Let me get in one last thing," Ray said. "We've been emphasizing correcting because it's so important, but correcting alone doesn't motivate people. Showing someone that he did something wrong and then showing him how to do it right won't *motivate* him to do it right. Or don't you agree?"

"I agree," Ellie said. "I've seen managers who think that the way to get workers to produce is to 'get on their case.' Some workers respond to that and won't do good work unless they are yelled at every so often—but they're a small minority."

"Put me down in the 'yes' column, too," Bobby Joe added. "Correcting is necessary, but it's a small part of motivation. I hope there's a good chapter on motivation in this book."

A QUICK SUMMARY

1. Make sure that every worker knows how he's performing. This is the manager's first responsibility where correcting is concerned.

2. Part of being a successful worker is to accept and use correcting, not fight it.

3. A new worker needs to know when he's doing well. Even workers who aren't new should be told occasionally that they're doing well.

4. Whether a worker is new or experienced, make sure he knows right away about any errors he makes. Don't wait.

5. A worker who is making errors needs to know:

   a. *What* he isn't doing correctly (or well),

   b. *Why* it isn't right, and

   c. *How* to do it correctly.

6. Showing a worker how to do something right usually means:

   a. *Telling* him what to do,

   b. *Showing* him how to do it, and

   c. Letting him *practice* doing it.

7. Sometimes it's not clear whether the worker made an error or not. A good sequence to follow in this situation is:

   a. Always discuss performance (and conduct, too) privately.

   b. Don't assume that you know what happened. Listen to the worker and communicate that you want to listen.

c. Try to reach an agreement on what happened.

d. If the worker didn't do anything wrong, make sure he realizes that you know he didn't. End the discussion.

e. If the worker did make a mistake, give him the chance to realize it.

f. If you have to point out the mistake, do it as objectively as possible. Don't blame or accuse the worker.

g. Then make sure the worker understands exactly what he did that was wrong, why it was wrong, and how to do it correctly. If necessary, go through the tell-show-practice sequence.

8. If possible, arrange the work situation so that individual workers find out directly how they are performing. The system should give you overall data, but not data on an individual's performance unless a worker is making repeated errors.

9. It's your responsibility to see that each worker knows the performance and conduct expected of him. It's his responsibility to produce them.

10. As important as correcting is, don't count on it to motivate workers.

StretchMeter 5: CORRECTING

1. I make clear to workers what I expect from them.

NEVER   1   2   3   4   5   6   7   8   ALWAYS

2. I get the facts before I decide whether a worker is wrong.

NEVER   1   2   3   4   5   6   7   8   ALWAYS

3. I deal with workers' mistakes objectively.

NEVER   1   2   3   4   5   6   7   8   ALWAYS

4. I am patient when correcting workers.

NEVER   1   2   3   4   5   6   7   8   ALWAYS

5. When I have to correct workers, I do it promptly.

NEVER   1   2   3   4   5   6   7   8   ALWAYS

6. I discuss sensitive subjects with workers privately.

NEVER   1   2   3   4   5   6   7   8   ALWAYS

7. I try to help workers to realize their mistakes for themselves.

NEVER   1   2   3   4   5   6   7   8   ALWAYS

Correcting ASAP

1. Effective correcting begins with being clear—or it doesn't begin at all. If you're reading this at work, put the book down, go to a worker, and check to see that he knows exactly how to do the most important part of his job. Over the next week, check with each worker at least once on some important aspect of the job. (If you're not reading this at work, do it as soon as you arrive.)

2. Before you decide whether a worker made a mistake or not, you have to get the facts. Make up your mind right now that you'll never tell a worker that he made a mistake until you're certain that's what happened. (Most of the time, you can't be certain until you've heard the worker's side of it.) To help you remember this in the situation, use a Reaction Alert (see the ASAP in Chapter 1 for details).

3. Perhaps you believe that workers make mistakes on purpose. Even if this belief is unconscious, it's harmful. To see the difference an objective attitude makes, tell yourself that for the next 30 days, you're *not* going to get "angry" or "disappointed" when someone makes a mistake. (If you need to, use a Reaction Alert—see ASAP 2.)

4. Some workers require a great deal of correcting before they begin to recognize their mistakes and take responsibility for them. It may help you to remember that correcting your workers is a key part of your job—not just something you're forced to do until you can get back to more important work. (ASAP 3 in Chapter 1 may be useful to you.)

5. Nothing is as easy, or as dangerous, as postponing correcting your workers. You just have to decide you're going to correct them, and then do it. Starting tomorrow morning, when a worker does something less than well, discuss it with him *immediately*. Do it for one week. Then another. Then another. . . .

6. Correcting workers in private shows them they have your respect. Unlike some changes, this one doesn't take much effort. Just *do* it.

7. Each of us would rather find our mistakes and correct them than have someone else point them out to us. Making a change

here can take some practice. Write yourself a note that says that when you have a performance discussion with a worker, you'll give him the opportunity to discover the mistake for himself. Then follow through. You may have some problems at first, and it won't work all of the time, but keep trying. It pays handsome dividends.

CHAPTER 8

Motivating

PHASE ONE MANAGEMENT	
Structuring	C
Selecting	O
Guiding	M
Correcting	M
Motivating	U
Delegating	N
Supporting	I
	C
	A
	T
	I
	N
	G

In this chapter, you'll find useful information on:

The importance of creating a work environment that motivates workers.

How to deal with workers who are motivated by different aspects of the job.

How to recognize critical motivators that are almost completely under the manager's control.

Would you be surprised to know that this chapter will help you develop workers who are motivated to do well? I didn't think you would.

WHAT IS EFFECTIVE MOTIVATING?

Interviewer: Ms. Martinez, we certainly appreciate your giving us this interview today.

Ms. Martinez: You're more than welcome.

Interviewer: Let me come right to the point. As you see it, what do we mean when we say a worker is motivated?

Ms. Martinez: A motivated worker is one who does willingly what the organization wants him to do.

Interviewer: That's interesting. And how do you motivate workers? Pep talks, motivational programs, free trips, threats, motivational courses, or what?

Ms. Martinez: Well, I don't use any of those. I try to set my workgroup up so that the best way for my workers to get what they want is to do what the organization wants them to do.

Interviewer: That's very interesting. But you must do some other things to motivate them. . . .

Ms. Martinez: No. Workers can only be motivated by themselves, not by me. I try to see that:

1. They get rewarded for doing good work, and rewarded even more for doing great work,
2. They never get rewarded for doing a so-so job, and
3. They never get penalized for doing their best.

   They do the rest.

Interviewer: That's part of it, but I'm sure there's more. Maybe you use motivational tapes, or sing company songs as do the Japanese, or . . .

Ms. Martinez: No, that's really all. And now, if you'll excuse me, I have work to do.

Interviewer: But. . . .

WHY IS EFFECTIVE MOTIVATING IMPORTANT?

Why was Anita Martinez so firm about not trying to motivate her workers?

First of all, she'd learned from experience that trying to "motivate" workers with pep talks, slogans, tapes, and all the rest brings only short-term success, at best. Sometimes these methods can recharge a workgroup or pull it through a bad time, but they never work over the long haul. These are all "external motivators;" reliable motivation comes from within.

Besides, when Anita put a lot of time and energy into trying to *motivate* her workgroup, she found she didn't have time to manage it. She got frustrated in a hurry, and this didn't do much for *her* motivation.

Anita was in a quandary, though. She knew that her workers needed to be motivated or they wouldn't get their work done. But if she spent all her time trying to motivate them, *her* job wouldn't get done. What was the solution?

At that point, Anita made a good decision. She talked with two of her best workers to get some feedback from their side. She found that the people in her group resented the motivational materials even more than she did. To her workers, the materials were insulting because they seemed to suggest that the workers wouldn't do a good job on their own. Anita discovered that her people *already* wanted to do a good job, but each for a different reason: job satisfaction, advancement, better pay, being part of a successful team, not letting her down, or something else entirely. The common thread of motivation was the work itself and the work environment.

That's when Anita got the message and changed her approach. Instead of "motivating" her workers, she used her time to see that their jobs brought out the best in them. As she spent less and less time on motivating, the workgroup performed better and better.

HOW DO I MOTIVATE EFFECTIVELY?

Anita Martinez: Look, I really need your help. You're my two best workers, and you're two of my best-motivated workers. I've tried and tried, but I just don't know how to motivate some of these people.

Tony Amico: You're a nice person and I like working for you, so I'm going to tell you the truth. We all wish you'd cut out the "motivational" stuff. I've heard those pitches dozens of times. As far as I'm concerned, they just take time away from doing the job.

Ernie Washington: Yeah, me too. If you had to depend on that cr . . . uh, stuff to get me to work, we'd all be up the creek.

Anita: Okay, I hear you loud and clear. But what do I do instead?

Ernie: For openers, you could forget all this rubbish about *you* having to motivate *us*. Pep talks might help keep us going in tough times, but that's about it. People get motivated by what happens to them on the job day after day—and that means you can be motivated not to do the job just as easily as you can be motivated to do it.

Anita: I'm not sure what you mean.

Reverse Motivation

Tony: I know what he means. When I first started here, over in receiving, I really wanted to do a good job. It wasn't hard for me to log in 25 percent more shipments that the standard. I did this for a few days, though, and the senior worker—a guy named Charlie—had little talk with me. He explained that what I was doing made the others look bad and that I should quit being a "rate-buster." I didn't like what he said, but the supervisor didn't seem to care, and the extra effort wasn't making me any more money. So, I slacked off—and I got along fine with the rest of the group from then on out.

Ernie: Yeah, I was in a group like that. We got a new supervisor, and he tried using this motivation stuff on us, too. Nothing happened. There just wasn't any reason for anybody to do more than we were already doing.

Anita: You mean that if you aren't paid for the extra work, you won't do it?

Tony: Nay, it's not that simple. The point is that Ernie and me and all the rest are going to do what makes sense for us. On those jobs we were talking about, it made sense to do what the others were doing. So that's what we did.

Ernie: Yeah—look at it this way. In those groups, people weren't producing their best for three reasons:

1. There wasn't any payoff for doing your best. As long as you logged in enough work to meet the standard, you got the same paycheck.

2. You actually got punished for doing your best. The way the group was set up, anybody who worked hard made everybody else mad. And the supervisor made it worse because he was always saying he didn't want any conflict.

3. You were rewarded for not doing your best. It kept you in good with the group, and it made the supervisor happy.

That supervisor was doing a tremendous job of motivating all of us—to do a so-so job. I left as soon as I could.

EXAMPLE: Reverse Motivation

"Tony, can I talk with you for a minute?"

"Sure, Charlie—what's up?"

"Tony, I know you want to do a good job, and we appreciate that. But you're going to get us all in trouble. You don't want to do that, do you?"

"No—but I don't know what you're talking about."

"You've been putting away too much material. What have you done the last couple of weeks—20 percent over standard?"

"About that, I guess. It isn't very hard to do."

"It may not be hard, but it's dangerous. Don't you realize that if everyone started working at your rate, management would make it the new rate. Then we'd all have to work that much harder just to get the same paycheck. You don't want that, do you?" Charlie clapped Tony on the shoulder.

"No, no I don't," agreed Tony. "But it seems to me that we ought to do as good a job as we can."

"My boy, you're just naive. What management wants is to get as much work out of us for as little money as possible. We're giving them what they're paying us for now—and the boys would be awfully upset if you screwed that up for everybody. . . . "

(WHAT IF Tony had kept on producing over standard? What do you think would have happened then?)

Anita: It still sounds to me like you're saying you should get more money if you do more than the standard. And don't get me wrong—I agree.

Limiting Motivation

Tony: Sometimes that's true, and sometimes it isn't. My last job was straight piecework. You produced 80 percent of the standard, or they fired you. If you turned out 110 percent or more, you got a bonus—depending on how much you produced.

Anita: That sounds pretty good.

Tony: It was, in a way. We did produce more. But the morale there was bad. People wouldn't work together. They were all working on their own rates, and to hell with anybody else.

You see, they didn't pay for anything except the number of pieces each person turned out that day. It didn't do you any good to help somebody else or try to help things in general. Most of us had ideas about how to do the work better, but we never told them to anyone. We figured that as soon as we did, management would put the idea into use, give the guy who came up with it a pat on the back, and raise the rate on us.

Different Strokes . . .

Anita: Okay, pep talks don't work, and extra pay for producing above standard doesn't always work. What does?

Ernie: The problem is that different people work for different reasons. Me and Tony, we really like being inspectors because it's an interesting job. We learn about a bunch of different products, and our work takes us through most of the warehouse. You'd have to pay us a lot more money to get us to take a job that wasn't this interesting. But if the job got boring, we'd leave.

Now Tomas, he's in it strictly for the money. He took the job to get the 35-cent-an-hour raise that came with it. He'll produce what he gets paid to produce, and he'll transfer out just as soon as he finds a job that pays better.

Tony: Here's another example. Mary and Reid don't care much about either the work or the money. Oh, they'd both move on if the pay got really bad or the work got too demanding. The reason they're here, though, is that they like the work environment. They like the people, and they like the fact that you're not hassling them all the time. They're going to give you whatever the group thinks is a fair day's work, so they don't cause any trouble.

Ernie: Let me give you two more quick examples: You've been having trouble with Arnold lately, haven't you? You know way? Arnold thinks you ought to answer a lot more questions for him. Bernice, though, would be out of here in a minute if you started butting in on her job. She wants to do it her way, and as long as she's getting it done she doesn't want *anyone* hassling her.

Anita: Wow! As well as I know all of you, I never realized all this. If I hear you right, you're saying that:

1. You and Tony are motivated because you like the work;
2. Tomas is motivated because we pay him well, and he doesn't really care about the work;
3. Mary and Reid work here not because of either the work or the money, but because they like the work environment;
4. Arnold isn't as motivated as he could be because he wants to lean on me more; and
5. Bernice only produces well if she's left alone to do everything her own way.

Tony: That's about the size of it.

EXAMPLE: Different Motivators

If you were to ask some of Anita's workers why they liked being in that unit, this is what they might say:

"It pays well," Tomas says. "I want to get a bass boat, and with this job I can afford it. My wife and I can afford to go out to eat at a good restaurant once a month."

"I really like the people here," Mary says. "We all get along very well, and it's a nice place to work. It's not tense, and the people aren't at each other's throats like they were at my last job."

"Well, I guess it's okay," Arnold says. "I think that Ms. Martinez ought to give us more guidance and help us more. I really don't think she takes her job as seriously as she should."

"This is the best job I've ever had," says Bernice. "Everybody stays out of my hair and lets me do my job. If there's anything I can't stand, it's a boss who keeps looking over your shoulder—and Ms. Martinez never does that. She's okay."

(**WHAT IF** Ms. Martinez began supervising everyone closely? How would Arnold and Bernice's reactions change?)

Anita: It sounds like an impossible job—trying to motivate such different people!

Ernie: As a matter of fact, you're doing pretty well. Everybody except Arnold is doing a good job. Look at what we've got:

1. Most of the people think the work is interesting even if they don't get as excited about it as Tony and me.

2. The pay is good. You do a good job of seeing that we get our bonuses when we earn them. Even if the rest of us don't work for money in the same way Tomas does, getting our bonuses on time makes us think that the organization appreciates our effort.

3. This is a good place to work. You've made some changes that make it more pleasant, we all get along well, and you're better to work for than a lot of managers. I've even heard Tomas and Bernice say they like being part of the group.

4. And you let us alone to do our work. I'd talk a lot more about that, except I have a feeling that the next chapter's going to get into that subject.

Anita: But what about Arnold? And I think Sandy feels the same way—what about him?

Tony: I'll tell you what I'd do. Mr. Purcell in shipping has a group of inspectors just about like us. And he's always telling his people what to do. I have two good friends over there who'd love to move over here. You could talk to Arnold and Sandy. If they really do want somebody to tell them what to do more often, maybe you and Mr. Purcell could do some switching. I remember reading not long ago that one of the rules for picking workers was that they should be comfortable in the workgroup—maybe a switch would make everyone happier.

Anita: Hey, you guys have been very helpful! Thank you.

Some Rules for Effective Motivating

Some time later, Anita told Frederick Holst, a good friend and manager of the purchasing agents, about her discussion with Tony and Ernie.

"That was good," Fred said, "but I'd like to add my five rules for motivating:

"*Rule 1* is: *Always notice a job well done.* You don't have to do anything elaborate: a pat on the back, a quick note, whatever. The important thing is letting the worker know that you're aware of and appreciate what he did.

"And notice that I said 'a job well done.' With a new worker, you want to give him an 'attaboy' even if he does just part of the job right. That's a job well done, for a new worker. It's either Mr. Johnson or Mr. Blanchard down the hall that has a great way of putting it: Catch a worker doing something right, and let him know you caught him.

"It's pretty much the same with an experienced worker who's been slipping. You want to notice any improvement (which is, by definition, a job well done), and you want him to know that you're noticed. Sometimes it's more difficult to learn to do good work again than to learn it in the first place.

"And, for heaven's sake," said Fred, "don't overlook the worker who *always* does well. Never take your good people for granted. They need to know you appreciate their continually good performance."

EXAMPLE: Noticing a Job Well Done

"Edna, that's the fourth report you've typed without an error. Fantastic."

"Molly, I just checked your drawings, and they're excellent. At the rate you're picking things up, you won't be a trainee much longer."

"Kareem, you've driven for two years without an accident. I've asked everybody to come in half an hour early on Friday so they can see you get your safety award."

"Paul, your sales for the month still aren't as good as they should be. That was the bad news. The good news is that you've improved 37 percent in the last three months. At this rate, you'll be back on target by the end of May. I think that's great—and I really appreciate the effort you're putting into this."

"I want to start our meeting by announcing that Mona's PC program for small purchases is going to be used in all 17 regions. She's done us all proud!"

(**WHAT IF** the manager hadn't noticed the job well done in each case? What difference would it make?)

"*Rule 2* goes along with Rule 1: *Always recognize people as quickly as you can after they've done a job well.* Do it right on the spot if you can. If not, do it as soon as possible. Our recognition program doesn't always help much—it usually takes anywhere from a week to three months to get a formal award through the system. I use it, but it's strictly secondary.

"When someone does something well, he feels good about it. When you notice him right away, it makes him feel even better. If you wait a week or a month, it's old news. By then, he probably won't have any feelings about it anymore—except maybe to be irritated that it took you so long to notice."

EXAMPLE: Quick Recognition

"Charlene, I saw how you helped Maurice with his packing just then. Teamwork like that is what keeps us on top—thanks!"

"I called you all together to tell you that an hour ago Beyta caught a purse-snatcher and held him until the police arrived. Beyta, I can promise you that you'll get an award for this—but I wanted everybody to know right away what a tremendous thing you did."

"Sam, I saw how hard you were working to make sure you had that connection right. Thanks—I really appreciate the extra effort."

(**WHAT IF** you were one of these workers? How would you feel about what the manager said?)

"*Rule 3* is a sort of reverse recognition: *People who aren't performing well should always be a little uncomfortable.* If a person is trying, recognize all of his improvements—but make sure he keeps the goal in mind. If he's *not* trying, push him to make a career decision. I don't mean harass him. But you might want to help him get a transfer or another job if he's not happy working for you. Whatever you do, never assure him that 'it's alright' not to perform well."

EXAMPLE: Keeping Poor Performers Uncomfortable

"Fred, I understand that you feel a lot of pressure to increase your output. Frankly, I think you ought to. It's important that everyone carry his share of the load."

"Jan, I realize the others aren't being very kind to you right now. In a way, I'm sorry. But they feel they're having to do most of your work, and I don't really blame them for being angry. I think if you show them you can do a first-rate job, though, you'll find things will change in a hurry."

"Marty, that's simply not acceptable work. I expect you to stay and redo it until it is."

(**WHAT IF** each of these workers feels comfortable with this level of performance? What happens to his performance?)

"*Rule 4* is the one we all tend to forget: *The recognition that one worker gets from another is very important.* I have a Gold Star program. When a worker does something that helps another get his job done, the person he helped gives him a Gold Star. Three Gold Stars let a worker go home two hours early on Friday afternoon. I really think, though, that for most of my people, just the good feeling from the Gold Star is enough.

"It doesn't matter what you use or how it happens. The important thing is to create a workgroup where the workers *want* to give each other recognition and know that you encourage it."

EXAMPLE: Workers Recognizing One Another

"Sarah, the way you've helped Charlie and me the last few days has been tremendous. I'm going to tell Mr. Jones that you should be Employee of the Month for sure this time."

"Ms. Peters, I just want everybody here to know that if it hadn't been for Wynona and Carlos's help on the Foster project, I never would have finished on time. They were really great."

"Mort, you've earned your wings this week. Mary Lou, Willie, and Laurie have all made a point of telling me how helpful you've been to them. I just want you to know I appreciate it, too."

(**WHAT IF** a manager keeps making note of the recognition workers give one another? What is likely to happen to their recognition of each other?)

"Rule 5 can be used to support every one of the first four rules: *Always work with your workgroup and the individuals in it to help them set improvement goals.* It's much easier for people to improve their performance— individually and together—if they have specific goals.

"Goals are funny things," Fred observed. "When people set goals, the goals themselves become motivators. You can almost say that a good goal *pulls* good performance out of people. And when someone achieves a goal, that's a logical place to recognize what he's done."

EXAMPLE: Encouraging Improvement Goals

"I've passed out to each of you cards that can be folded to fit in your pocket. Page one has the company goals. Page two has the division goals on it, and page three has our branch goals. I want each of you to put your two or three most important personal goals on page four. I'll drop by and talk with you one-on-one Monday and Tuesday to see what you've got. We've discussed them before, but if you need any help before then, come see me."

"Red, I know how hard it is to get back in gear when no one's pushed you for good performance in a long time. I know you can do it—that's why I persuaded Mr. Emmert to keep you on. But you need to set some clear performance goals for yourself. I don't expect you to do everything at once—but I want you to draft some realistic monthly goals and discuss them with me at nine o'clock Friday morning."

"Bernadette, you're the most consistent producer I have. Would you be willing to work with me on a couple of goals for this coming year? I'd like to see you develop your presentation skills so that you could give the monthly update instead of me."

(**WHAT IF** Bernadette didn't want to work on presentation skills?)

"What's most important about all the rules is that they're things *you can control*," Fred emphasized. "They don't depend on the organization's recognition program or pay system or anything else. *And* they're real things that matter to workers."

"I sure do thank you." Anita said. "Before I forget all these things, I'd better make myself . . ."

A QUICK SUMMARY

1. Managers don't have time to do their other jobs and keep "motivating" workers, too.

2. In fact, workers can only motivate themselves. They will only do what makes sense to them. If they think that doing above-average work will get them into trouble, they will be motivated to do mediocre work.

3. It's the manager's job to create a work situation where doing what the organization needs is what makes sense to workers. This means that workers:

   a. Get rewarded for doing good work and rewarded even more for doing great work,

   b. Never get rewarded for dong a so-so job, and

   c. Never get penalized for doing their best.

4. Different people are motivated in different ways. Here are some of the most common motivators:

   a. The work itself,

   b. The pay,

   c. A pleasant work environment,

   d. A pleasant and helpful manager, and

   e. The freedom to do the job one's own way.

5. A good manager tries to know the main motivators of each of his

people, and to create a workgroup that is motivating in as many ways as possible.

6. Although a manager can't always control everything that motivates his people he can control some very critical motivators by:

a. Always recognizing a job well done,

b. Always recognizing people as quickly as possible after they've done well,

c. Always relating whatever is being recognized to good performance,

d. Never letting workers who aren't performing well be comfortable with their performance,

e. Encouraging workers to recognize each other for cooperation and teamwork, and

f. Encouraging workers, and working with them to set improvement goals constantly.

StretchMeter 6: MOTIVATING

1. I try to create a work situation that motivates my workers

NEVER   1   2   3   4   5   6   7   8   **ALWAYS**

2. My workers are rewarded only if they do a good job.

NEVER   1   2   3   4   5   6   7   8   **ALWAYS**

3. My workers are encouraged to do their best without penalty.

NEVER   1   2   3   4   5   6   7   8   **ALWAYS**

4. I understand what motivates each of my workers.

NEVER   1   2   3   4   5   6   7   8   **ALWAYS**

5. I recognize a job well done.

NEVER   1   2   3   4   5   6   7   8   **ALWAYS**

6. I recognize workers quickly for what they do.

NEVER   1   2   3   4   5   6   7   8   **ALWAYS**

7. I relate all recognition to good performance.

NEVER   1   2   3   4   5   6   7   8   **ALWAYS**

8. I see to it that poor performers are uncomfortable.

NEVER   1   2   3   4   5   6   7   8   **ALWAYS**

9. I encourage workers to recognize each other.

NEVER   1   2   3   4   5   6   7   8   **ALWAYS**

10. I encourage workers to set improvement goals.

NEVER   1   2   3   4   5   6   7   8   **ALWAYS**

Motivating ASAP

1. If the work situation doesn't motivate your workers, they probably won't be motivated. Look at the five different kinds of
   motivation that Anita, Tony, and Ernie were discussing. Which
   one of them can you influence most quickly? Within the next
   week, make at least one change that will make this more of a
   motivator. Keep making changes, with this motivator and the
   others. Don't ever stop.

2. Workers have been rewarded even if they didn't do a good job?
   Starting now, begin to change this. If you're rewarding them
   for less than good performance, stop it! If your boss is rewarding them for less than good performance, get him to stop it!
   Whatever you have to do, stop it!

3. If workers are penalized for doing their best, stop it! All of the
   comments in ASAP 2 apply.

4. If you truly understand motivation, you understand that each
   of your workers is motivated individually. Get a small memo
   pad or notebook, and label a page for each worker. For the next
   week, listen carefully, ask discreet questions, and identify *at
   least* one motivator for each worker. Use that as basic training.
   Keep identifying motivators from now on.

5. Do you still believe that workers ought to do good work without any recognition? No one (including yourself?) wants to be
   taken for granted. For the next week, make a point of identifying and recognizing *at least* one instance of good performance
   each day. Try to recognize good performance with each worker
   at least once during the period. Then keep at it—until you retire.

6. It's easy to put off recognizing workers. In fact, the recognition
   programs of many organizations encourage such procrastina-
   tion because they take so long. For the next week, recognize at
   least one worker each day immediately for a job well done.
   Then keep doing it. (A warning: Don't be phoney in your recognition! If you can't find something you can genuinely recognize, don't recognize anything. If you can't honestly praise a
   person, don't praise him. If you honestly can't find anyone or
   anything to praise in your workgroup though, you are in serious, serious trouble. Either you need to change workgroups or
   they badly need to change you.)

7. Remember, the name of the game is performance. Make a note: The next time you're going to recognize someone for something other than performance, you're going to relate it to performance. You can't? Then you should ask yourself whether this is really something you want to recognize.

8. You should cultivate a genuine empathy with your work–group—but don't feel sorry for nonperformers. If you have any nonperformers and they aren't uncomfortable, it's time to change that. Don't pick on them, or embarrass them, or freeze them out. Just make sure they're not quite happy with their performance. Start now. (A word of caution: Many workgroups have individuals who aren't world-beaters but who take care of the jobs that someone has to do. If you have someone who can't produce like the others but who does these jobs well, he may not be a nonperformer. The key is whether your best workers see him as "getting by" without having to produce. If the answer is "yes," you have a nonperformer.)

9. If your workgroup is successful, your workers ought to be recognizing each other constantly. If they're not, you need to intervene. Ask: Are they helping each other? If they're not, you have work to do to make the group fully successful (see Chapter 12 for more information on that). If they are, you need to notice and encourage the times when they recognize the help they give each other.

10. Improvement goals are amongst the great motivators. Sit down tomorrow morning and sketch out a plan to help your people develop some. The plan should include: (1) making clear to your workers what improvement goals are and why you want them, (2) helping them set realistic goals and timetables, and (3) discussing their progress with them. Then implement the plan. (Another word of caution: Don't approach this plan as something to be forced on your workers, but as an opportunity for them to become even more successful.)

CHAPTER 9

Delegating

PHASE ONE MANAGEMENT	
Structuring	C
Selecting	O M M
Guiding	U N
Correcting	I C
Motivating	A
Delegating	T I
Supporting	N G

In this chapter, you'll find useful information on:

The three basic principles of delegating.

The rules for successful delegating—including the five levels of delegation.

How to let workers solve their own problems.

Delegating encourages workers to take responsibility for their jobs. *It also helps* motivate them to do well. *When you delegate fully, you find out if your workers know* what to do, how to do it well, *and* when they've done it well.

WHAT IS EFFECTIVE DELEGATING?

K ay Ishikawa has strong opinions about effective delegating:

"Effective delegating is a way of harnessing the energy of your people that can't be matched.

"Some managers think that workers are there simply to do the jobs they're hired to do and follow directions. In my experience, workers are too well educated and self-aware to accept this kind of treatment. It doesn't recognize the hidden abilities workers have, and it treats them as though they were machines.

"A really effective manager educates his workers by passing along his knowledge and experience to them by guiding them on the job. Just to make them smarter? No. His real goal is to produce self-sufficient workers. When the workers have reached that state, and they know the manager's basic policy, the manager can then simply delegate authority to them and let them handle the job.

"Will the workers make mistakes? Of course. The mistakes they make, though, are a small price to pay for the growth you can expect in your workgroup. Delegating allows workers to make full use of their abilities. People aren't like machines; they like to use their heads. Delegating unlocks your workers' unlimited potential.

"But you need to remember that effective delegating requires clear thinking. You delegate only what you can *effectively* delegate. If the worker is fully successful, you let him do the job without interference from you. If he isn't completely successful, you don't delegate quite so much. But you always delegate, and you always push your workgroup toward being more responsible, having more authority.

"If you do it carefully and thoughtfully, if you build up your workers' trust in you and let them use their abilities, they'll produce first-class work for you willingly."

WHY IS SUCCESSFUL DELEGATING IMPORTANT?

Earline Walton knows:

"When I put myself into the shoes of the people who are working for me, I know that the more freedom I'm given and the more opportunity to be creative I'm given, the more I'm going to enjoy my job and want to come to work. And I'll do a better job when I'm there.

"I didn't always manage that way. I'd hang over people's shoulders to see that they were doing everything just right. Then I realized all the attention and effort I was giving them was teaching them to be dependent on me rather than to rely on themselves. That was valuable learning for me. Now I make whatever I need very clear, and I make it clear that they can do it. In other words, I let them be successful.

"Besides, I don't have time to do their jobs or their thinking for them. If I let myself get tied down that way, I wouldn't have time to do what really matters to me. I would keep them from being successful, and I'd keep myself from being successful, too. No thanks!"[1]

HOW DO I DELEGATE EFFECTIVELY?

"Amelia, this idea of delegating really makes me nervous."

"Why, Bill? Delegating can be tricky, but you don't need to be scared of it."

"Mr. Jankowski was just talking with me about delegating. He said I should delegate everything I can to my workers. I'd like to do that, but I'm afraid of what might happen. I know my people too well. They just couldn't handle it."

"Couldn't handle it, Bill? Why?"

---

[1]Although the other speakers in this book are not based on specific individuals (their names are made up, and they're composites of many people I've known,) that's not the case with Kay and Earline.

The words of "Kay Ishikawa" are based on those of Kaoru Ishikawa, one of the foremost Japanese experts on quality control. Much of what Kay says is paraphrased from Mr. Ishikawa's book *What Is Total Quality Control? The Japanese Way,* translated by David J. Lu (Englewood Cliffs, NJ: Prentice-Hall, 1985).

"Earline Walton" is a fictitious name, but much of what she says is paraphrased from an interview in Jim Wall's book *Bosses* (Lexington, MA: Lexington Books, 1987). The person being interviewed is the manager of a bordello.

I thought that if you knew that two people as different as this believe so strongly in delegation, you'd take it seriously, too!

"They're just not ready for it. They don't know the jobs well enough yet."

The Basic Principles of Delegating

"Bill, if you want to be successful at delegating, you have to keep three principles in mind:

1. Your primary goal is to delegate to your workers responsibility and authority for their work. You've got to be clear about this, and you've got to communicate it clearly to your workers. Until you've done so, they won't be successful workers and you won't be a successful manager. In fact, you can almost say that the reason you do structuring, selecting, guiding, correcting, and motivating is so that you can delegate successfully. It's that important.

2. You always delegate what people are ready to handle—keeping in mind that you want to keep stretching them a little. There's something of a knack in knowing just how much to delegate when, but you'll pick that up.

3. You need to keep tabs on your delegations. When you have a completely successful worker who takes full responsibility for his job, you can delegate and not worry about it. Anything less than that, though, and you need to make sure that the delegation gets completed—and completed right."

EXAMPLE: How *Not* to Delegate

"Broderick, we're glad to have you with us. You need to understand right off that I know this business better than anyone else, and I make the decisions around here. If you're good at listening and doing what you're told, you'll get along fine."

"Gosh, Mr. Abel, I have a couple of ideas about how we might . . . ."

"Not necessary—just follow instructions and everything will be fine."

"Frampton, I know you've only been with us a short time, but I need someone to take this project and run with it. Here's a brief sketch of what needs to be done. You take care of it for me, okay?"

"Gosh, Ms. Baxter, I don't really understand what some of this is about. . . ."

"You'll do fine. I know you'll figure it out. Now go handle it, and let me get on with my work."

"Darn it, Celecia, I was really counting on you to have this done. I know that today is the date I mentioned to you."

"I remember clearly, Mr. Cleve, that you said that you'd like for me to *try* to get it done by today. I did try, I really did."

"I should have known—if you want something done right around here, you have to do it yourself! Give it to me, and I'll take care of it."

(**WHAT IF** you were the boss of Mr. Abel, Ms. Baxter, or Mr. Cleve? What would you say to them?)

"Your three principles of delegation sound good, Amelia, but I'm not sure just how to apply them."

The Rules of Delegating

"Believe it or not, Bill, it isn't that hard—if you set your delegations up right and follow through on them. I was reading a manual for new managers the other day that offered a good set of rules for delegation. Are you interested?

"Of course."

"Okay, here they are—

Rule 1: When you delegate, be very clear about what you're delegating. It might help you to think about the five levels of delegation:

    a. *Complete delegation:* Use this with a fully successful worker. You tell him what you want done, give him the due date, and then leave it up to him. The only thing he owes you is to tell you when he completes it.

    b. *Substantial delegation:* Use this with a good but not completely successful worker. You tell him what you want done and when the deadline is, but this time, he reports back to you *before* the work is finalized. The worker has a great deal of freedom, but you also get the chance to discuss what's going to be done before it actually takes place. This level of delegation has two time targets: (1) the date by which the worker will report to you on his plans for the project, and (2) the date by which the project will be completed.

By the way, when you make a substantial delegation, it means that you intend for the worker to make the necessary decision. You allow yourself a final chance to look at the decision, but both you and the worker should assume that the decision is still his. If you have reservations about the worker's decision, discuss it with him—in hopes that one of you will persuade the other. Don't overrule the worker's decision unless it's absolutely necessary. If you intend to make the decision yourself, start out with a limited delegation, not a substantial one.

c. *Limited delegation:* Use this with a worker who is good but even less successful than one who would rate a substantial delegation. You tell him what needs to be done, and he gets back to you with recommendations. You're going to make the final decision. In this case, the time target isn't when he will complete the delegation, but when he will give you the recommendations. Then you set the final target, depending on the recommendation you choose.

d. *Minimal delegation:* Use this with a new worker or a poor worker who's improving. Never accept this level of delegation for a worker as a continuing situation. At this level, you assign the job *and* tell the worker how to do it and when to do it. His only responsibility is to do what you tell him on schedule. In this case, you may also set up some dates by when you want progress reports from him.

e. *No delegation:* Avoid this whenever you can. This is the level where you tell the worker that you'll decide whether you want something done, and if you do, you'll get back to him. That leaves the ball in your court and takes any initiative away from the worker. In this case, there aren't any time targets at all."[2]

---

[2]I've borrowed heavily here from William Oncken's book *Managing Management Time* (Englewood Cliffs, JN: Prentice-Hall, 1984). It's a super book, and it's mentioned in "Your Own Management University" at the end of this book.

EXAMPLE: Levels of Delegation

"Meyer, Marketing needs a new projected sales report. Hanna Jenks in the Analysis Branch knows what they need. Get together with her and set it up for them. Let me know when you're finished." (**complete delegation**)

"Meyer, Marketing needs a new projected sales report. Go talk to Hanna Jenks in the Analysis Branch and find out what they need. Work out your design, and get my calendar to go over it with me next Friday. As soon as you talk with Ms. Jenks, let me know if you think it'll affect any of your other priorities.'" (**substantial delegation**)

"Meyer, Marketing needs a new projected sales report. See Hanna Jenks in the Analysis Branch and find out what they need. Figure out three or four different ways we could get the information for them, and get back to me next Friday." (**limited delegation**)

"Meyer, Marketing needs a new projected sales report. I want you to talk with Hanna Jenks in the Analysis Branch. Find out exactly what she wants: the purpose of it, how much detail, how often—the works. Get the information to me by Thursday. After I've had a chance to look at it, I'll let you know what I want you to do." (**minimal delegation**)

"Meyer, I understand that Marketing wants a new projected sales report. I may need you to do something with it, and I'll let you know if I do." (**no delegation**)

(**WHAT IF** you were Meyer? How would you feel about each delegation?)

*Notice that at the complete level the manager didn't mention priorities. That's because he expects Meyer to identify any conflicts in priorities and see that they get resolved. (This can happen either because Meyer resolves them or, if appropriate, lets the manager resolve them) Below that level, the manager makes sure that conflicting priorities get resolved.

"I want to ask you some more about Rule 1, Amelia, but I think I understand the basics. What's next?"

"Rule 2: Be sure every delegation has a specific time target. This may be the date by which it's to be done or the date by which you want a progress report or recommendation. But never let a worker walk out of your office with an assignment that doesn't have a clear time target. In fact, for everything except complete delegation or no delegation, you would set a specific day and time for getting back together with the worker.

EXAMPLE: Setting Specific Time Targets

"Tvet, this special order needs to be out of here by ten o'clock tomorrow morning."

"Barney, find a way to schedule this job in so that it can be done by April 17. Have Ada put you on my calendar for three o'clock tomorrow afternoon so you can tell me how you intend to do it."

"Henrietta, you know all about Acme's requirements for its new computer system. I want to draw up at least three alternative configurations for me to review. See that Mike puts you on my calendar no later than next Wednesday morning. You can give me the alternatives, and then I'll make a decision."

"Muncie, these are the changes that have to be made in the Pioneer estimate. Have the revised estimate in final form to me by three o'clock this afternoon."

(WHAT IF you had to delegate a project to Sandra, a new worker? What level(s) of delegation would you consider?)

Rule 3: Make it clear that time targets are to be met. It is *not* acceptable for a worker to walk in the day something is due to tell you it won't be done on time. All workers are capable of thinking ahead and keeping track of dates. Whenever a worker sees that a target time is going to be missed, he should get with you at least several days in advance to discuss the situation. Anything else is completely unsatisfactory.

EXAMPLE: Seeing That Time Targets Are Met

"Wesley, it really breaks my heart to have to mark your project Unsatisfactory."

"That can't be right, Mr. Bergman. I gave you everything you asked me for."

"You did indeed—but you gave it to me a day late."

"For heaven's sake! It was just one day, and I had other things I had to do, too."

"That doesn't matter. The rules we run by are perfectly clear. You had an assigned project, and you were late; that automatically makes it unsatisfactory work, and that's how it's going down on the books. If everything you do for the next month is on time, I'll consider upgrading it. Miss one more deadline without working it out with me beforehand, and this stays 'Unsatisfactory' forever."

(**WHAT IF** Mr. Bergman said "It's really 'Unsatisfactory,' but I'll overlook it this time? What would this communicate to Wesley?)

Rule 4: It's never your responsibility to follow up to 'see how it's going.' This is the clearest symptom of poor delegation; it's really a form of 'pestering.' In the first place, it keeps the worker from being responsible for the delegation. Good workers will resent the follow-up, while poor workers will depend on it. Also, it you feel you need to follow up, it probably means you're not comfortable with the degree of delegation you made—or that you neglected to set realistic time targets. Any way you look at it, it's a mistake.

EXAMPLE: The Consequence of "Following Up"

"Emily, I thought your project was due today."

"Oh my goodness, Mr. Dvorak, it is, isn't it? Why didn't you remind me of it sooner?"

"I shouldn't have to remind you of . . .. Oh, Tom, how are you coming with the internal review summary?"

"Glad you asked. I've been working on something else, and the summary just slipped my mind. I'll get right on it."

"Please see that you do, Tom—it's important to get things done on time, you know. Now, Emily, back to your project. When do you expect to have it done?"

"Well, I can work on it tomorrow afternoon. . . ."

"Excuse me a moment, Emily. Rifaat, how's the quarterly projection coming?"

"I haven't started it yet, Mr. Dvorak. Remind me of it again on Tuesday, will you?"

"I'll see if I can remember, but you really ought to . . . oh, never mind. Now, Emily, back to you."

"Excuse me, Mr. Dvorak, but I have to get some papers together that I promised Mrs. Hurst I'd deliver to her yesterday. Could you please catch me later this afternoon?"

"But I . . . but . . . but. . . ."

(**WHAT IF** Mr. Dvorak started insisting that everyone meet his own deadlines without "follow-ups" from him? How do you think his workers would react initially?)

Rule 5: You and the worker share the responsibility for understanding what's to be done. You should be specific, and you should check to see that he understands just what you want done. But the worker must take responsibility for understanding and must ask you for more information when he needs it. If the worker ends up doing something different from what you wanted, you're both at fault."

EXAMPLE: The Consequences of Misunderstanding

"Arinda, where are the pads I asked you to order?"

"I'll get them for you, Mr. Phillips. I picked them up at supply on my way into work this morning."

"How in the world could you carry three gross of pads?"

"Three *gross*? I thought you wanted me to get three pads!"

"Yes, ma'am—right on schedule."

"What's this mess?"

"It's the proposal. Didn't you want to see it in draft?"

"Draft? It's due in final form in Mr. Linkletter's office in half an hour."

"Gosh, Ms. Abrams. I'm really sorry, but I'm sure you told me you wanted to see a draft by this afternoon."

(**WHAT IF** you were Mr. Phillips or Ms. Abrams? What do you do now?"

"That sounds good, Amelia, but I'm not sure I see just how to do it."

Some Practical Tips

"Okay, let's practice it. I'm working for you, and you want me to do a price survey and buy a new copying machine for you. How would you do that as a complete delegation?"

"I think I understand. I'd say, 'Amelia, I want you to get us a new copying machine. Be sure you find the best price and try to get it here by about January 1.'"

"Good beginning, but you made two mistakes. First of all, you didn't tell me what kind of copier you want. If I'm a good worker—and I am, because you're making a complete delegation—I'll ask you for more details. But I really shouldn't have to do that. You should take the lead there.

"Second, you never delegate to someone to 'try' to do something, and there's no such date as 'about January 1.' If you mean 'I want you to purchase one and have it here by January 1,' say that. If you mean 'I'd like you to have it by January 1, and if you can't, tell me by December 15 when you can have it,' tell me that. Even if it's a complete delegation, don't leave the time target fuzzy. Does that make sense?"

"Yeah, Amelia, I see what you mean. Let me try another one."

"This time, let's say you want to accomplish the same thing, but you want to make the purchasing decision. How would you do that?"

"I'd say, 'Amelia, we need a new copier. I'd like to upgrade what we have, and I want to know what's available. Look over the market for a good buy and get back to me with your recommendation by December 15. On your way out, ask my secretary to put you on my calendar for then.'

"Now I know I would have given you a lot more details and probably discussed any models that I had in mind with you. Can we just pretend I did that?" asked Bill.

"Okay—and this time you did well. I have a pretty clear idea of what you want me to do, and I know exactly when I need to have it done. The only thing I don't have is a good understanding of the range of alternatives you want to consider. You may want me to recommend one machine, or you may want to pick from three or four. It would be helpful for you to give me that information."

"I understand that—it makes sense."

"One more thing, Bill. Let's suppose that I walk in on the morning of December 15 and tell you I need another week. I've just had too many things piled on me. . . ."

"Whoa right there. That's when I'd put my correcting hat on and you and I would have a little heart-to-heart. I see what you mean about missing a time target. If I really needed that copier by January 1, I'd be in deep trouble."

"Exactly—and that's why you have to insist that people notify you in advance when they can't meet a time target. If you're expecting something to be done, and then you find out at the last moment it's going to be delayed, your planning is shot. You just don't let workers do that to you."

"Thanks, Amelia. I think I have the picture now."

Delegating Problem Solving

"You do, Bill, but I want to make one other point, and that's about problem solving. When they interviewed you for the management job, did they ask you how you were at problem solving?"

"They sure did. I don't think I'd have gotten the job if I hadn't convinced them I'm good at it."

"I expect you are good. And if you're not careful, it's going to foul you up."

"Huh? What do you mean, Amelia?"

"Bill, what's your reaction if one of your workers brings you a problem?"

"Generally, I try to solve it for him on the spot. If I can't, I work on it for a day or two. If it can be solved, I can usually work it out by then."

"Okay—what does the worker learn from that?"

"He learns that I can be depended upon to solve problems."

"True. Doesn't the worker also learn that he can dump problems on you and not have to worry about them any more?"

"No, of course not . . . hmmm . . . I guess you're right. I do end up solving most problems for my people."

"They're really delegating upward, aren't they?"

"Wow! I never thought of it that way, Amelia. I guess so. Now that you put it in those terms, it doesn't sound like such a good thing for me to do."

"It isn't. Not only do you let them delegate work to you, but you keep them from learning how to solve problems themselves. If you have successful workers, you do something even worse: You keep the most interesting part of the work for yourself."

"You've made a believer of me," Bill said—"but how do I stop?"

"Basically, you delegate problem solving to your people. Your worker may be able to solve a given problem on the spot; often, when a worker turns to you for a solution he already has one and is hoping you'll ask for it. If he can't solve it, delegate the problem at a level you're comfortable with and treat it like any other delegation. You'll be helping to create a successful worker, *and* you'll keep some unnecessary work off your desk."[3]

EXAMPLE: Keeping Problems Where They Belong

"Mr. Anselm, I have a problem with the automatic feed on my machine. It keeps jamming."

"Have you tried to fix it?"

"Well, I checked for debris in the gears, but they're clean."

"What do you think is causing the jamming?"

"Well, Henry said that when he had this problem with a machine, it had something jammed back under the cam."

"Do you think you could check that?"

"Yeah, I think so. If that doesn't work, is it okay to take the cover off and check the shaft? . . ."

"Ms. Emory, we have a real problem. Supply will only send us two boxes of diskettes a week, and we're using almost three times that many. Can you talk to them?"

"Maybe. Have you tried borrowing disks from another section?"

"We've already borrowed everything we could find, and we've recycled all of our disks that don't have current data."

"Okay. I want you to draft a letter to Supply for me to sign. Give them the facts on what we're using and ask for whatever amount of diskettes you think we need. After I sign it, you can take it down there and work something out with them. . . ."

---

[3]It's important to have your common sense up and running here. There are some problems you should solve. If a worker comes in and says "Charlie and Max are fighting in the break room" delegation probably isn't the appropriate response.

The touchstone you should use is whether the problem is directly part of your responsibility as a manager. If it isn't, delegate it. If it is, handle it—unless delegating all or part of it would help develop the worker.

"Ms. Chastain, I have a problem. Tony Carlos keeps asking me to help him with his work, but he never wants to help me with mine."

"What would you like to do, Elaine?"

"Tell Tony to help me."

"Do you think he would like that?"

"It doesn't matter whether he likes it or not. He ought to help me!"

"Tell you what I'll do, Elaine. I'll get together with you and Carlos right after lunch. You can tell him what you think, and we'll see what the two of you can work out. . . ."

(**WHAT IF** Ms. Chastain had agreed to talk to Carols for Elaine? Who would have delegated to whom? Who would have gotten the blame if things didn't go the way Elaine wanted?)

"I'm really glad I ran into you Amelia, but I don't want to forget anything. Do you mind if I try to summarize what you've said?"

"Not at all, as long as it's . . ."

A QUICK SUMMARY

1. There are three basic principles of successful delegating:

    a. Your primary goal is to delegate to your workers responsibility and authority for their work. Neither you nor your workers will be successful unless this point is clear to everyone.

    b. You should delegate only what people are ready to handle. This includes making delegations that stretch your people a little each time.

    c. You must keep track of your delegations and know their outcomes.

2. There are five basic rules for successful delegating:

    a. Be clear about what you're delegating. This is where the different levels of delegating come in. You can delegate completely, substantially, partially, minimally, or not at all.

        1. Complete delegation means telling the worker what to do and by what date to have it finished. He will only report to you that the work has been completed—he has made the

final decision.

2. Substantial delegation is like complete delegation, except that you want the worker to see you *before* he takes final action. That way, if he is not doing what you think should be done, the two of you can discuss the situation before a final decision is made.

3. Limited delegation means telling the worker what needs to be done and asking him to make recommendations to you. You make the final decision.

4. Minimal delegation means telling the worker how to do the job and when to do it. You shouldn't let anyone operate on this level for long.

5. No delegation means telling a worker that you'll decide whether you want something done and get back to him. Avoid this level whenever possible because, otherwise, you end up with all the work.

b. Be sure every delegation has a specific time target. This can be the date by which it's to be done or the date by which you'll get a progress report or recommendation.

c. Make it clear that time targets will be met. If they can't, the worker must get back to you in plenty of time, not at the last minute.

d. It's never your responsibility to follow up and see how a worker is doing with his delegation.

e. You and the worker share the responsibility for understanding what's to be done. This doesn't mean that you get off the hook if you're not clear about what you want, but a good worker must make sure he knows what you want.

3. Let workers solve their own problems.

StretchMeter 7: DELEGATING

1. My goal is complete delegation to each of my workers.

NEVER   0   1   2   3   4   5   6   7   8   ALWAYS

2. My delegations are challenging to my workers in a helpful way.

NEVER   0   1   2   3   4   5   6   7   8   ALWAYS

3. I see that the delegations I make stay under control.

NEVER   0   1   2   3   4   5   6   7   8   ALWAYS

4. I use whatever level of delegation is appropriate.

NEVER   0   1   2   3   4   5   6   7   8   ALWAYS

5. I put specific time targets on all delegations.

NEVER   0   1   2   3   4   5   6   7   8   ALWAYS

6. I insist that time targets be met.

NEVER   0   1   2   3   4   5   6   7   8   ALWAYS

7. I set levels of delegation that don't require me to "pester."

NEVER   0   1   2   3   4   5   6   7   8   ALWAYS

8. My workers make sure that I'm clear when I delegate.

NEVER   0   1   2   3   4   5   6   7   8   ALWAYS

9. When workers bring me problems, I let the workers solve them.

NEVER   0   1   2   3   4   5   6   7   8   ALWAYS

10. My goal is complete delegation to each of my workers.

NEVER   0   1   2   3   4   5   6   7   8   ALWAYS

Delegating ASAP

1. If your goal as a manager isn't complete delegation to your workers, neither you nor they will be as successful as possible. Sit down with a notebook or several sheets of paper—one for each worker. Write down the highest level of delegation you're comfortable making to the first worker. Then list the obstacle(s) to delegating more completely to him. Now, put down at least one step you'll take immediately to start removing the obstacle(s). Continue for each worker.

2. You can fail to challenge your workers helpfully in either of two directions:

   You may be too conservative, and not delegate as much responsibility as they're ready to take. If this is what's happening, do the exercise in ASAP 1.

   You may be delegating more responsibility than your workers can handle right now. (You know this is happening when you have to keep interfering to see that they get things right.) Doing ASAP 3 will help with this. (And remember that the purpose of increased delegation is to challenge your workers—not intimidate them.)

3. Not making careful, controlled delegations is as harmful as not making delegations. Review the five levels of delegation. Then make a page for each worker (as in ASAPs 1 and 2). Determine the highest level of delegation you can give that worker and still be confident you have the delegation under control. Limit your delegations to him to that level—until you can develop that worker (again, see ASAPs 1 and 2).

4. Review ASAPs 1, 2, and 3. One of them will help you select more appropriate levels of delegation.

5. When you don't put specific time targets on all delegations, you're setting the worker *and* yourself up for failure. Review the levels of delegation to see what time targets are appropriate at each level. Starting tomorrow, don't make a delegation below the complete level without setting a *specific* time at which the worker is to get back to you for the next step. Do it, without exception, until it becomes second nature.

6. Once time targets are set, they must be met. If you've been letting your workers fail to meet targets, call a meeting tomor-

row. Tell your people that you're sorry you've been letting them down that way and explain that now you've seen the light. Let them know that, as of the end of the meeting, deadlines must be kept—period.

Your group won't love you for this change, but you and they will function more effectively because of it. (If you can't think of anything else, explain to them that the change will build character.)

7. You don't have to "pester" when you make realistic delegations. Refer to ASAP 3.

8. It's your responsibility first to see that you're clear about what you want when you delegate, but it's in your worker's best interest to help you in this. The next few times you delegate to a worker, encourage him to ask you for all the details he needs. Stress that you want to be clear and you need his assistance. If you're honest about it, this technique will help.

9. When you solve problems for workers, you let them effectively delegate upward. Like Bill, you may need a Reaction Alert (see the ASAPs for Chapter 1). Put a ball right in the middle of your desk to remind you that when one of your people walks in with a problem, the ball stays in his court. Either he solves it on the spot or he walks out with it as a delegation. You can help him with the problem—if that's appropriate—but see that you don't take over the problem.

10. See ASAP 1. The question is important enough to repeat.

CHAPTER 10

Supporting

PHASE ONE MANAGEMENT	
	C
Structuring	O
	M
Selecting	M
Guiding	U
	N
Correcting	I
	C
Motivating	A
Delegating	T
	I
Supporting	N
	G

In this chapter, you'll find useful information on:

How important it is to support your workers.

How to convince your boss that your workers are successful and that *you're* successful.

How to protect your workers from harassment without "rescuing" them.

This chapter will help you develop successful workers by seeing that they have the tools and supplies that they need. It will also explain how to support workers so they will consistently take responsibility for their work and be motivated.

WHAT IS EFFECTIVE SUPPORTING?

Phillip McDonald (bangs on the vending machine until the bag of potato chips falls to the tray): You know, I'm getting burned out on Chris as a supervisor. He gives us all this jazz about doing a good job and then won't get us the stuff we need to do it.

Roger Degarnier (gets a cup of coffee from another machine and heads for a table): That's a shame. Evelyn's just the reverse. She's a real change from our last boss, Kellar. I used to have to fight like crazy to convince him that we needed new revisions of our drafting software. Now all I have to do is explain to Evelyn what a program will do, and she does her darnedest to get it for us. And you're right—that does make it easier to to a good job.

Phillip: I don't think the idea of helping us out ever crossed Chris's mind. We've been trying for months to persuade him to try to get us some better quality paper. It's useless—we're still using the standard junk that misfeeds more often than not.

Roger: Oh, I'm glad we don't have to put up with that. Evelyn gets us what we need and then stays out of our way. She comes by once in awhile and asks how I'm doing. If I don't have a problem, I say, "Fine." Then we talk for a little bit, and she goes on to someone else.

Phillip: It would be great if Chris were like that. He gives us something to do, and then he keeps looking over our shoulders while we do it.

Roger: It sure helps when someone believes you're smart enough to do a good job and doesn't hassle you. You know, I think the thing I like the most is the way Evelyn keeps the flack off us. Charlie Tuttle, from design, came over here the other day and started telling me how to lay out my drawings. Before he got two sentences out, Evelyn came up—and the next thing I knew he was in her office. Later, she came back and asked me to make a couple of small changes. I was glad I didn't have to deal with Charlie and his temper.

Phillip: If anyone comes by our section yelling at us, Chris disappears. It's as bad here as it was down in the lab. Down there, half a dozen people were telling me how to run the tests. When I'd complain to Elsie, she'd just tell me to give people what they wanted. Some days I'd run the same test three different ways for three different people!

Roger: It helps when you get you orders from one person.

Phillip: I'd be grateful if Chris just stopped second-guessing us. About a year ago he had me negotiate a procedure change with R&D. I did it, but then Mr. Baker showed up over here with steam coming out of his ears—yelling about the new procedure we'd worked out. Chris flew out of his office and started yelling at me right along with him. Neither one of them paid any attention to what I had to say. Chris and Barker agreed on a different procedure right there— right there, without even asking me why I'd done it the way I had! Then Chris had the nerve to tell me to make the change and have it on his desk in an hour.

Roger: From what you say, I feel like giving Evelyn a medal. I remember shortly before she let Adrian go, when Adrian was making a lot of dumb mistakes. Evelyn tried and tried to get Adrian to change, but it was no use. Even then, Evelyn never let anyone from outside the section get after Adrian or tell her what to do.

Phillip: You're lucky to have a manager who does such a good job of supporting her people. Your only problem is, she's so good she's probably going to get promoted out of her job. Chris never will!

WHY IS EFFECTIVE SUPPORTING IMPORTANT?

Harold Ramsey learned quickly why it's important to support workers effectively. The first week on the job, he gave Ozzie McIntyre a special-purchase order and told him to expedite it. Ozzie did it, told Harold he had done it, and went about his business. Then Juanita Massey, who'd ordered the item, complained to Ozzie that the order wasn't what she'd wanted. Before Ozzie could answer, Harold walked up, apologized to Juanita for the fouled-up order and promised it wouldn't happen again. Then he took Ozzie into his office.

Ozzie, who was eligible for retirement, didn't feel he had to put up with anything from anybody. As soon as he was in Harold's office, Ozzie closed the door and turned on Harold in a rage.

"Don't you *ever* do anything like that again, or I'm out of here! I won't have you overruling me and embarrassing me in front of anybody—anybody!"

"Well, If you'd done it right," Harold replied angrily, "I wouldn't have had to do it! You know how important it is to keep our customers happy."

For the next five minutes, the two men had a shouting match. Things were going from bad to worse when Harold had the presence of mind to say, "Look, this is getting us nowhere. I'll shut up for a minute if you will, and then maybe we can talk about it." Ozzie glowered at him, but nodded. They sat down and looked at each other for a minute.

"Okay, Ozzie, I want to find out just what's eating you. If you'll stop yelling, I'll keep my mouth shut and listen."

Ozzie nodded, and told him: "Look, I know that wasn't just what Juanita wanted. But you told me to get the order expedited. It would have taken me four days longer to get her what she requested. So I did what you told me and bought the other."

Harold started to say something about pleasing customers again when he suddenly realized what Ozzie had just said. He grinned sheepishly, "I guess you did exactly what I asked you to do, didn't you?"

That got things back on an even keel, and Ozzie and Harold talked for quite a while. Then they got to the heart of the matter.

"Look," Ozzie said, "if you trust me enough to give me a job to do, then you ought to trust me enough to support what I do. At least you ought to listen to why I did something the way I did. You're the boss— I don't have any problem with that—and I like it when you let me use my own judgment. But I'm not going to do it if you're going to over-rule me without listening to my reasons."

Harold did listen. When Ozzie left the office, both he and Harold felt good about their talk. As a matter of fact, Ozzie stayed on and worked for Harold for another five years before he retired. For his part, Harold learned some very important things:

1. The most important thing Harold learned was that if he expects employees to be successful, he has to give them the support they need. Without Harold's support, Harold's workers lose the motivation to be fully successful, and he loses credibility.

2. Harold learned that his workers were only behaving realistically. Without the right tools or supplies, without Harold's support, without protection from outside flack—his workers would waste tremendous amounts of time. It simply isn't worth it for them to take responsibility under those conditions.

3. And Harold learned that if he's going to manage the workgroup, he has to provide the support. It's important that the workers look to him and trust him to get them what they need and keep the flack off them. He has to make sure that other managers don't harass his people or give them work direction.

HOW DO I SUPPORT EFFECTIVELY?

Mary Ellen Zdenek: All right, you've read the chapter on supporting your workers, and we've spent the afternoon discussing how important it is. Now I want to know what you've gotten out of the book and the workshop that you're going to take back to the job.

Chris Turley: Frankly, I'm a little shaken up. I thought I was doing a decent job of supporting my people—but now I'm not so sure. The problem is I'm just not sure I can trust them. I can't support them unless I can count on them to do things right.

Evelyn Kee: It sounds to me like you need to go back and work on delegating effectively. I don't have any idea how good your workers are, but I know that if *you* don't think they're successful, you'll never support them properly. And you'll never know how good they are unless you delegate to them and see what happens.

Maria Vela: I'm going to work at delegating, too, but there's something else I'm going to do as well. I can see now that my work-group needs to know what my philosophy is and how I want things done. There are lots of ways of doing things that are "right" in a vacuum, but they don't fit the way I want my people to do things. If I'm going to support them, I need to know in advance that what they do will be consistent with our overall approach as a team.

EXAMPLE: Communicating Your Philosophy

"Wynetta, let me say one thing right off: I'm very happy with the way you handled the joint report with Purchasing. I need to talk with you a little about it, but I want you to know that I'm not being at all critical."

"Mr. Ermina, that sounds like you're getting ready to zap me good."

"I'm sorry if it sounds that way because I'm not. In fact, what I want to do is to make up for a mistake on my own part. There's something about doing a joint report that I forgot to tell you."

"Okay. . . ."

"After you brought the report back to get it typed, you had a couple of good ideas that you had Ellen include in the final draft. The first time Purchasing saw those changes was when you took the final copy to them for signature."

"Yes, but they liked the changes."

"I know, but we can't count on that every time. One of the principles I always follow in a joint project is never to make a change unless both areas have agreed to it."

"I know that's good practice," agreed Wynetta, "but we were running late on the report, and I didn't want to hold it up."

"I understand your reasoning, but the principle is more important. We've spent a lot of time building up trust between us and the other sections. Part of that trust involves a promise that we won't even *appear* to do anything behind anyone's back."

"But I . . ."

"I know—you didn't intend to go behind Purchasing's back, and I don't think they took it that way. But you don't know how things were around here a couple of years ago when no one trusted anyone else. I don't want to do anything that might remind people of those days. And I know you don't want to, either."

"Oh, no—I really like the way we get along."

"We all do—so I want everyone in my section to be completely open in everything. Sure, it would have taken you a little longer to run those changes by Purchasing before you did the final copy. But it's important to take that time, and I want you to do it in the future."

"All right—I understand. The next time you give me a report to do, I'll make sure all changes get coordinated."

"Thank you. You're a good worker, Wynetta, and I really appreciate your flexibility. . . ."

(**WHAT IF** Mr. Ermina had just criticized Wynetta for not coordinating the changes? What do you think Wynetta's reaction would have been?"

Max Jaros: For me, I need to work on keeping out of my workers' way. They're good, and I've been interfering too much with them. I need to spend more time making sure that they get the supplies they need. We've had to go light on packing materials for the last two weeks, and several of my people have been complaining that they can't do a good job that way. I was out on the line, trying to help them—but I should have been finding out why there's a problem with the packing stuff and fixing it.

Managing Your Boss

Evelyn: I think my biggest problem is my boss. He keeps wanting me to get involved in everything. If I tell him I've delegated some project and I know it'll be done right, he gets upset and insists that I get him a status report on it. Then when I ask the worker about the job's status, he gets upset because I don't trust him.

Maria: I used to have the same problem. Maybe your boss doesn't see you as a fully successful manager yet. If he'd read this book, he'd be working with you to make you successful. It doesn't sound like he is, so you've got to prove to him that you're successful. Tell me, do you make sure he knows it when one of your people does a particularly good job?

Evelyn: No, not really. I thought the idea was for him not to have to worry about my group.

Maria: You don't want him to worry about it, but I think you do want him to know how good it is. If you make it a point to keep him posted on your people's successes, he may start to realize how good they are. Then he won't have the same problem when you delegate fully to them.

Chris: Hey, that might work with formal recognition, too. I've never thought about it before, but when you give a worker an award for doing a good job, you're not just saying something to him. Other people—like your boss—see it, too. Of course, you can only pass out awards if your people earn them. . . .

EXAMPLE: Showing Off Good Workers

"Toni, it gives me great pleasure to recognize you as the Employee of the Month for our division. You're the third worker from your section to get the award in the last six months. I think that speaks well for you and your co-workers."

"Thank you, Ms. Feldman. It's a real pleasure to work in the division."

(A few minutes later.) "Well, Wilson, you did it again. Sometimes I think you have something on the judges."

"Not at all, Ms. Feldman. Frankly, it's all the result of that management course you sent me to about a year ago. What I learned there started me thinking about how capable my people really are. Each one of them who has won the award won it strictly on his own merit. I keep telling you how good they are; maybe now you'll start believing me."

"I must admit, Wilson—you've become quite a salesman. But, I still find it hard to believe they're as good as you say they are."

"Let me tell you a secret. Do you remember how pleased you were with that design for the annual report? Well, Toni did that one."

"I expected you to do it yourself."

"I know. And if Toni hadn't done a good job, I would have—you don't ever need to worry about that. The point is that she did a super job. Neither you nor I needed to add a thing to it."

"Still, something that important . . ."

". . . Needs to be looked at carefully. I know that, and it was. It took me a while to realize it, but I have three or four people in my group who turn out first-rate work every time. Why should I waste my time looking over their shoulders or only give them the easy stuff to do while I take all the challenging material? Be honest, now, Ms. Feldman—have you ever had such consistently good designs coming out of the shop before?"

"I hate to say it, but no. Your people *are* good. . . ."

(**WHAT IF** Wilson had never mentioned that Toni did the design for the annual report?)

Evelyn: It sounds funny, but if I understand all this correctly, one of my jobs is to convince my boss to make a complete delegation to me where my people are concerned. I've never thought of it that way.

Mary Ellen: That's a good insight. Remember, you're part of your boss's workgroup. Everything we've said about successful workers applies to you, too. You must show your boss that you know what to do and how to do it; you must have access to the proper tools with which to do it; and you must be certain that you and your boss agree on what constitutes doing your job well. Your boss needs to see that you're motivated and that you take responsibility for what your workgroup does.

Max: Yeah—this is all part of building up our credibility. Our bosses have to know that when we say we'll do something, we will—and that we'll do it well and on time. That's the only way we can keep them out of our hair.

Sarah Tillman: That's what I've been thinking about while I've been listening to all of you. My boss likes to get involved with my workgroup. She comes down to the section once or twice a day. If I'm there, we usually talk a little and she goes away happy. If I'm not, she'll find something about what my people are doing that she doesn't like and she'll tell them to change it. Then my workers get confused and don't know which way to do it.

Maria: I think we've all had that kind of boss, and it's a tough problem. If you tell your folks to ignore your boss, you'll really get into trouble. But if they listen to him, you end up in just as much trouble. This is what I do: I tell my people to listen and make sure they understand whatever my boss is saying. Then, if they can, I ask them to hold off on *doing* anything differently until they check with me. That way, I get a chance to try to change my boss's mind if I don't like what he's done.

Max: That's a good idea. Tell me, Sarah, does your boss know how you feel about the way she goes around you to correct your people?

Sarah: To be honest with you, I've been afraid to bring it up. You've almost convinced me, though, that I need to talk to her and deal with this one head-on. My boss is pretty sharp; I think there's a good chance she'll listen.

EXAMPLE: Managing Your Boss

"Mrs. Cuellar, may I speak to you for a moment?"

"Certainly, Sarah—what's on your mind?"

"I don't know just how to put this. I hope what I have to say won't offend you."

"That bad, huh? Okay, let me have it."

"It's not *that* bad . . . it's just that . . . well . . . you keep telling my people what to do, and they're not sure which one of us to listen to."

"Sarah, I *am* their boss—and yours."

"I know you are, and so do they. Besides, it's not a question of disagreeing with what you say—we honestly want to do things the way you want them done. That's not really the problem, though. May I give you an example of what I mean?"

"Certainly," said Mrs. Cuellar.

"When you came by this morning, Gloria was classifying the warranty repairs. You stopped her and told her to change several of the classifications—remember?"

"Yes, I do, Sarah. The way she was doing it wouldn't have provided the kind of breakdown that the analysis group needs."

"I understand. Once Gloria told me what she was doing differently, I saw why you made the change. It does work better. The problem is that I'd told her to do it one way and then you came by and told her to do it differently. Gloria didn't know what to do; she was afraid she'd make one of us mad no matter what."

"That's unfortunate, but the repairs must be broken down the way I told her."

"Agreed. Remember, I'm not trying to argue with you about how to do the job. We *want* to do it your way. May I make a suggestion about how we could handle situations like this?"

"Go on."

"When you see a problem with the way someone in my workgroup is doing something and I'm not around, could you just ask the person to stop what he's doing and move on to something else until you have a chance to talk with me? Then you can tell me how you want it done, and I'll see that the worker makes the change. Then the worker won't have to worry about whom he takes instructions from or whom he might make mad."

"Okay, Sarah. I'm willing to try it a time or two because I don't want to upset your people—but only if it doesn't hold things up."

"That's all I ask. I promise you, Mrs. Cuellar—I'll make it work. . . ."

(**WHAT IF** Sarah hadn't said anything to her boss? Would it have affected Gloria's attitude toward Sarah as her boss?)

Protecting Workers

Furman Wright: It's not my boss that's my challenge in supporting my people—it's my customers. The organizational analysts all work for me, and they make a lot of decisions that aren't very popular.

Not a week goes by that I don't walk into the office and find some other manager chewing on one of my people."

Sarah: I get some of that, too—probably we all do. How do you handle it?

Furman: Very carefully. On the one hand, I do delegate completely to most of my people. If they make a decision, I expect them to be able to defend it. I'm not about to rush in and try to rescue them; that's not good for anybody.

On the other hand, I absolutely will not tolerate someone abusing my people, particularly the newer ones. Just as soon as another manager begins to yell—and particularly if he starts getting personal—I take over. When my people become managers, they can put up with that; until then it's my job to protect them from that kind of abuse.

Maria: Good for you! I wish more managers felt that way. When you're a good worker and somebody in management starts chewing on you, it's hard to know what to do. Because I've had some first-hand experience with that situation, I try my best to keep my people from ever getting caught in it. If I can't do that for them, none of the rest seems to matter much.

EXAMPLE: Preventing Abuse

"Damnit, Tim, you know I needed an answer today on that new function! I won't put up with this kind of garbage!"

"Mr. Wilson, I keep trying to tell you . . ."

"You keep trying to make excuses to me! I'm sick and tired of little wimps like you who think they can tell me what to do. Every one of you thinks they're better than the people who . . ."

"Sam, why don't you come into my office?"

"Damnit, Furman, keep out of this."

"No! I don't know what's going on here but it's completely inappropriate for you to talk to Tim that way. If you'll come with me, we can . . ."

"We can nothing—I've got some more things I want to say to your boy here."

"Well, you'll just have to go without saying them. Tim, why don't you take a break and step across the hall for a minute. Now,

Sam, do you want to talk here or in my office or in my boss's office? . . ."

(**WHAT IF** Sam had wanted to go to Furman's boss's office? What approach should Furman take there?"

Mary Ellen: Very good—I can see that you all understand what you've read and that you've listened to each other. Let me see if I can capture the heart of it for us.

(She turned to a fresh sheet of paper on the easel and wrote . . .)

A QUICK SUMMARY

1. Important points in the chapter on supporting:
   a. If you expect your employees to be successful, you have to give them the support they need. Without that support, they lose motivation and you lose credibility.
   b. Employees are being realistic when they refuse to take responsibility without effective support.
   c. There's just as great a payoff for you. If you can't get your workers what they need, keep the flack away from them, and prevent other managers from giving them orders, you lose the ability to manage them.
2. Important points in the discussion:
   a. We must develop successful workers. We can't support them fully unless they're good.
   b. We must see that our workers know what our philosophy is and how we want things done.
   c. Once our people are successful, we need to stay out of their way. Our time should be spent supporting, not interfering.
   d. It's vital that workers have the right tools and supplies.
   e. We must convince our bosses that we're fully successful members of their workgroups. Until we do this, they'll continue to deny us the freedom we need to support our people effectively.
   f. We can improve our credibility by seeing that our bosses know when our workers do a good job. Recognizing workers formally also helps.
   g. We need to persuade our bosses not to give our people orders

directly, but to go through us. If we don't, we put our workers in uncomfortable situations.

h. It's our responsibility to protect our workers from abuse by others without trying to "rescue" them from defending their own actions.

Maria: "May I try and summarize the whole thing in one sentence?"

Mary Ellen: "Certainly. Here's the marker."

Maria wrote:

In other words,

If you want your people to take responsibility for what they do, you've got to support them when they do it.

Everybody agreed.

StretchMeter 8: SUPPORTING

1. I support my workers even when things are tense.

NEVER   1   2   3   4   5   6   7   8   ALWAYS

2. My workers are so good that I can easily support them.

NEVER   1   2   3   4   5   6   7   8   ALWAYS

3. My workers know what my philosophy is.

NEVER   1   2   3   4   5   6   7   8   ALWAYS

4. My workers have the supplies they need to be successful.

NEVER   1   2   3   4   5   6   7   8   ALWAYS

5. My boss believes I'm a successful manager.

NEVER   1   2   3   4   5   6   7   8   ALWAYS

6. My boss gives orders to my workers through me.

NEVER   1   2   3   4   5   6   7   8   ALWAYS

7. I protect my workers from abuse.

NEVER   1   2   3   4   5   6   7   8   ALWAYS

8. I let my workers deal with honest criticism themselves.

NEVER   1   2   3   4   5   6   7   8   ALWAYS

Supporting ASAP

1. Workers take with a grain of salt what you say when things are going well. They believe what you say—and do—when the going gets tough. This one is a piece of cake: all it takes is intelligence and guts! Before you make any delegation, ask yourself, "Am I willing to support whatever this worker does?"[1] Make the fullest delegation you can and still answer "yes." That's intelligence. Then, delegate and support the result, no matter what. That's guts.[2]

2. The key to effective support is developing workers whose work makes supporting them easy. If you haven't done that yet, review the last six chapters and do the relevant ASAPs.

3. Passing on your philosophy to your workgroup is critical, but you don't have to call it a "philosophy." At the next six meetings you have with your full workgroup—no less often than once a month, surely—discuss some aspect of getting things done that's important to you. You might choose topics like "listening to customers" or "the importance of careful proofreading" or "why the machinery needs to be spotless." The only requirement is that it must be something you genuinely care about and want your workers to practice.

4. No worker should have to do a job with inadequate tools, equipment, or supplies. If your people are hampered in this way, it's time to make a change. Compile a list of the four tools, pieces of equipment, or kinds of supplies that they need the most. Work on the first item on the list until you've arranged to get what your people need. Then do the second, then the third, then the fourth. After that, see what else remains. From then on, never let the list get longer than one item.

[1]Remember that "whatever this worker does" varies with the level of delegation. If it's complete delegation, you've committed yourself to his decision—it's going to be your decision. With substantial delegation, you get a final shot at it before it goes out. If it's minimal delegation, you control both the decision and its implementation. Picking the appropriate level of delegation is the key.

[2]Remember, too, that supporting a worker doesn't mean that you uncritically accept what he does. If the end result isn't what you wanted, it's time to put on your correcting hat—but in private. Supporting the worker means that in public you fully support his action—and, if it has to be changed, you make it possible for the worker to change it.

5. It's not impossible to be better than your boss thinks you are, but it is hard. For the next four weeks, point out at least one accomplishment of your workers to your boss each week. Two or three would be better. If you can't identify at least one accomplishment a week, go back to Chapter 8 and proceed from there.

6. It's challenging but necessary to find a way to keep your boss from giving orders to your workers directly. The example in this chapter is one approach; there are dozens of others. Choose one, and pursue it for the next few days or weeks. Make it clear to your boss that you want to cooperate fully—but that you also want to be the one who tells your workers what to do. While you're waiting for your boss to change, make sure that each worker knows to tell you as soon as he can whenever he gets instructions directly from your boss.

7. Your workers don't get paid to take abuse. You should believe that down to your toes and *practice* it. If you haven't been practicing it, right now is just barely soon enough to begin. (Note that when Furman couldn't redirect Sam Wilson in the example in this chapter, he made it impossible for Wilson to continue being abusive by sending Tim away.) Whatever the means, put yourself between your worker and the abuser and stay there. It's all part of having the guts mentioned in ASAP 1.

8. The other side of sheltering workers from abuse is letting them learn to deal with honest criticism. If you tend to jump in just because they're being criticized, stop. If it's a deeply ingrained habit, use a Reaction Alert (see the ASAPs for Chapter 1).[3]

---

[3] We're talking about trained workers here. Naturally, you don't make new, inexperienced workers defend themselves along. The more you can let a worker carry the ball, though, the better. Then you can limit yourself to providing "moral support" and reinforcing his responses.

CHAPTER 11

Communicating, Part I

PHASE ONE MANAGEMENT	
Structuring Selecting Guiding Correcting Motivating Delegating Supporting	C O M M U N I C A T I N G

In this chapter, you'll find useful information on:

Being open and honest.

Being clear.

Listening.

Good communication skills are absolutely essential for developing successful workers. All managerial activities—structuring, selecting, guiding, correcting, motivating, delegating, and supporting—depend completely on effective communication for success.

WHAT IS EFFECTIVE COMMUNICATING?

"Well," said Helen Washington, "here we are."

"Yes, and we'd better get down to business," Clarice Kersey responded. "Imagine, giving us two hours to write an entire chapter."

Larry Malone grinned. "What's new? We never get enough time to do anything else. Why should this be different?"

"Then let's stop talking about it and *do* something," Fred Bernstein said. "I think communicating is the most important skill for a manager to have, and I think we ought to start there."

"You won't get any argument from me." The last speaker was Paula Macias, who had driven in from the suburban office. "Structuring, selecting, guiding, correcting, motivating, delegating, and supporting are all important—but if you can't communicate well, you can't do any of them effectively. Does everybody agree with that?"

They all nodded.

"I agree," Helen said. "Frankly, I didn't want to come to this meeting. But now that I'm here, I think that first of all an effective communicator is open and honest. It wastes too much time when people have to guess at what you're really after."

"But don't overlook clarity," Clarice added. "Everything needs to be put clearly and simply, whether you're speaking or writing."

"I heard what you said," Larry joined in, "and I think you both made important points. I'd like to add listening responsively to openness and clarity. If we're really going to communicate, I need to hear what you're saying—and I need to *show* you that I'm hearing it."

Fred nodded. "I'm hearing some very constructive ideas from the group. I'd like you to consider a fourth one: using feedback. It's hard to manage well if you can't give people an objective evaluation of what they do or say."

Paula leaned forward in her chair: "That's all well and good, but you're still missing something important. You've got to get in there and just persuade people sometimes. I believe in the value of being persuasive, and I'm sure each one of us sees its benefits."

WHY IS EFFECTIVE COMMUNICATING IMPORTANT?

"Have you ever stopped to think," Charlie asked, "just how critical communicating is? There's not a single management activity that is effective unless the manager communicates effectively. Can you imagine trying to guide or delegate if you're not being clear, or correcting someone if you can't give objective feedback?"

"That's very true," Helen commented, "and it's true at every step. If a manager isn't open and honest, for instance, workers spend a tremendous amount of time trying to figure out what's really going on. Several years ago when I worked in a district office of another company, there was a lot of talk about a reorganization. Our manager wouldn't tell us anything, so we assumed that we were about to lose our jobs. Each one of us started looking for another position, and a couple of people actually left. Then we found out that the reorganization wasn't going to touch the district offices. It was never the same there again, though, and I left a couple of months later."

"I'd like to make a speech about how important being clear is, but I don't think I have to," Clarice said with a smile. "Let me try something else. Raise your hand if you *haven't* had a worker do something wrong in the last two months because you weren't clear about an assignment."

No hands went up. "Case closed."

"We've been talking about the output side of communicating," Larry added, "but don't forget the listening side. One frequent complaint I've heard from workers over the years is 'My boss won't listen to me.' That really bothers people. I'll bet each of us has had the same problem with our own bosses." Almost everyone nodded. "I thought so. What do you do when your boss won't listen?"

"I'll tell you what you do," said Paula. "You stop talking. What good does it do you to tell someone something you think is important if he won't listen to you?"

"Exactly. Nothing else works if the person isn't listening."

Fred leaned forward: "I find this very useful, and I'd like to add something to it. Effective communicating requires listening, alright, but that's not enough. You also need to feed what you hear back to the person speaking. That way, you can check to make sure that what you heard is what the other person said. If the two of you don't use feedback, you may have completely different ideas—yet think you're agreeing."

"Like that old Abbott and Costello routine, 'Who's on First?' At the end, they agree, but each of them is saying something completely different." Helen grinned as she mentioned it.

"Yeah, I remember that. But there's more. If you don't give feedback to workers on what they're saying and doing, they never know when they make mistakes," Helen said emphatically. "When I took over my section two years ago, there was a guy in it who I was told was incompetent. I did have to spend some time working with him, but in a matter of weeks he improved to a fully satisfactory rating. Do you know what the real problem was? Nobody had ever told him that what he was doing wasn't okay. And I've seen the same thing time and time again—all from lack of feedback."

"I don't want to argue with any of you," Paula said as she gestured vigorously, "but you're still leaving out something critical. Where would any of us be if we weren't persuasive? What do you do when being open and clear fails—fire the poor worker? Not me, anyway. I'd certainly rather try to persuade him to do things my way. Wouldn't you each agree that persuasion is a critical part of communicating?"

Everyone nodded, and then Helen added, "Paula, I know how important you think persuasion is—and I think it's important, too. But we have to be careful not to rely on it in isolation. Combined with openness, responsive listening, and feedback, it's very useful. But if you try it without the others, you can get yourself into a situation where you don't know what's going on in your own workgroup."

Paula began, "Now wait a minute. . . ."

"It's okay, Paula," Fred interrupted. "Helen thinks persuasion is important, just like the rest of us. It's just that by itself, persuasion is all one way. A manager who's always pushing his own ideas doesn't hear what workers are trying to say. Problems that might otherwise surface stay hidden because people believe the manager isn't interested. It's not that persuasion doesn't matter—it's just that it needs to be part of an overall balance. Right?" He looked at the others. They nodded emphatically, and even Paula agreed.

HOW DO I COMMUNICATE EFFECTIVELY?

"You're right," Paula said. "I know how important these other qualities are. It's just that I had it drilled into me that I had to be a good salesperson in order to be a successful manager. Now I know that's not enough, but it made such an impression on me that it's still the first thing that comes to mind."

Being Open

"Yes, I remember that seminar," Helen said with a wry smile. "They should have put us through it *after* they told us about everything else.

If there's one thing I think I've learned, it's that you can't be an effective manager if your people don't trust you. And they're not going to trust you if you're not open and honest with them."

Larry joined in, "You bet! I wrestled with this a long time myself. I had the idea that because *I* was the manager *I* was the one who had to have all the answers. I never let my workers know if I was having problems, and I never admitted it to them if I was wrong and they were right. When I finally gave in to the obvious and just started being myself, if made all the difference in the world."

"Yes, being open to what others have to say is very important," Helen said. "It's a part of the listening that Larry was talking about, but it's a part of openness, too. It means you have a real give-and-take with your workgroup and let yourself change. Do you know the remarkable thing about all this? If your workers realize you're willing to change, they become a lot more willing to change themselves."

Fred nodded: "That's good. I think I heard you say that openness means:

1. Being yourself and not playing some kind of role. You let your workers in on what's happening inside your head. If they ask questions, you give them the most honest answers you can. That way, they can trust what you say and don't have to second-guess you.

2. Being receptive to what your workers have to say and willing to take them seriously. If you have to change some of your ideas, that's okay. Your goal is what's best, not what's 'yours.' When your people see that you're open to them, they can be open with you—which makes it easier for them to change if that's necessary.

"Did I get it right?"

"You certainly did," Clarice said enthusiastically, "but if this is going to be part of a book for managers, I think we need to add something here. If you inherit a workgroup that's not accustomed to honesty and openness, don't expect them to change overnight. Be as honest and open as you can and give them the chance to be the same. But give them some time to see that they can really trust you. Be patient and consistent, and they'll come around."

"I agree. It took a very long time for my group to communicate openly," Helen said, "but it was certainly worth it."

EXAMPLE: Being Open

"I'm sure that our managers will do what's best for us. Now let's just forget our questions and put in a good day's work."
or
"I don't know whether we'll be affected by the district office consolidations. Frankly, I'm as concerned as you are. I promise you, I'll let you know if I find out anything."

"It's not up to you to question my decisions. If you get to be a manager someday, you can make the decisions. Until then, just do it my way."
or
"I realize that my approach on this may not be the best. But right now, it's the best way I know to get it done. If someone has another idea that we could implement quickly, I'm willing to listen. If not, I expect you to do it this way."

"Okay, here are the objectives and the milestones for the Mendoza project. I expect everyone to get his part of the job done on time. Now let's get to work."
or
"Here's a draft of the plan for the Mendoza project. I want each of you to look at the part that you'll be working on and let me know by this afternoon whether or not you think the milestones are realistic. We'll get back together as a group tomorrow morning to iron out the details."

(**WHAT IF** you took the first option of each pair of examples? What would the workers' reactions be? How would they be different if you chose the second options?)

Being Clear

"Yes—there's no substitute for openness. In a different way, being clear is just as important. When I first came to work here, I thought I would never understand all of the technical terms and acronyms we use. Then one day, soon after I became a manager, I was explaining what we do to my first new hire. My initial reaction to the blank look on her fact was that she wasn't as smart as I'd thought. Then I realized I was using all the jargon that had given me so much trouble in the beginning, and that's when I became a convert to clear, simple English."

Paula nodded emphatically. "Amen! Nobody ever confused anyone by speaking and writing plain English. I get so fed up with the bureaucratese we write around this place. Just once I wish someone would say 'used' instead of 'utilized' or would just come out and recommend something, rather than 'it is recommended that. . . .'"

"Amen to your amen. I think being clear and simple is so much a part of being open and honest. How in the world can someone trust you when you sound like an operations annual?" Helen grimaced as she said these last two words.

"Do any of you ever compose your letters out loud before you write them?" Larry asked. Several of the others nodded. "I'm glad I'm not alone. It really helps me put my ideas into simple English, but I thought maybe I was being weird."

"Not at all," Fred said intensely. "Getting rid of jargon, speaking simple English, saying your sentences out loud before you write them—anything that will help you be clear is good. Do you know what I discovered the other day? When Ms. Jenks, the division chief, has a letter she's sending to all the employees, she gives it to the person who delivers the in-house mail and asks him to tell her what it says. If he can't understand it, she rewrites it. That's what she thinks of clarity and simplicity!"

EXAMPLE: Being Clear

"We received your letter, subject as above, and considered the suggestions therein carefully. Our analysis reveals that the proposal which you bring forward, while not without considerable merit, does not integrate well with our current strategy."

or

"Thank you for your letter suggesting that we use videodiscs to advertise our products. It's a good idea, but we just can't use it right now."

"Charlie, you know that we think very highly of you around here and appreciate the numerous contributions you've made to the organization. However, I've been evaluating your production for the past few months, and while there are many, many instances of satisfactory production—indeed, some even better than satisfactory—there are also some instances, some few instances, of, shall we say, somewhat-less-than-satisfactory performance. While I don't want to exaggerate the importance of these, it does appear that . . ."

or

"Charlie, you don't usually make mistakes, but you've been making a lot of them lately. Why?"

"Our next award goes to a lady who embodies in herself the fine traditions that we have always tried to uphold here in the division—initiative, perseverance, innovation, and a full commitment to her job. Its difficult to find the words to express my admiration for her accomplishments and the high regard in which I hold her contribution to our organization. It is an honor, though, to be able to stand here today and recognize her sterling contribution to the success we've enjoyed over the past few months. I'm referring, of course, to . . ."

or

"Our next award goes to Nancy Weedam, who spearheaded the 30 percent productivity increase we've had in the last six months. I want her to come up here and tell us how she did it. . . ."

(**WHAT IF** you had just landed here from an alien planet? Would your intergalactic translator be able to unravel the meaning of the first statement of each pair in this Example?)

Listening

"Well, we certainly agree on the importance of clarity. Now if only the person who puts what we say into the book can make it clear to the readers. . . ."

"Yes," Larry commented. He paused a moment, then continued, "You know, though, whoever does that is at a real disadvantage because he can't hear what we're saying. Once we write down the words, all the nuances fall out. It's to our advantage that we work so closely with our workgroups. We can actually *listen* to them instead of having to read about what they think and feel, which sure makes a difference."

"Yes," Paula agreed, "but only if you let the person *know* you're listening. A worker can't see inside your mind, so you have to show your interest. If you lean back in your chair, fold your arms, and just say 'Hmmm' every so often, he'll never believe you're paying attention—no matter how carefully you're listening. You've got to lean forward, make eye contact, and respond to what the worker is saying if you want to show you're really listening."

"That's valid," Helen said, "as long as no one gets the idea that you have to do those particular things." Paula started to interrupt, but Helen continued, "No, no—I know you didn't mean that. We just need to make sure that whoever reads this knows that there are any number of ways for a manager to communicate that he's really listening. You know, something so simple as a raised eyebrow or a small gesture can show someone you're with him."

Larry looked at her and nodded. "Exactly!—anything that shows you're really listening is okay. And don't forget to ask questions. You learn a lot more that way, and you communicate that you're interested in what the worker is saying. Besides,"—a sly grin crept over his face—"there's no better way to keep somebody from feeding you a line than to keep listening and keep asking questions."

"I had a beautiful example of that just yesterday," Fred said, grinning back at Larry. "Some of you know Frenchy Modisette over in Section A. Well, he came over here raising Cain about a report we'd done on a joint project. I didn't think he had anything to complain about, and I darned near told him so. But I kept listening—and asking questions—and finally the real problem came out. He thought we hadn't given him enough credit for some of the research he did. That was easy enough to change, but if I hadn't held on and listened, I'd never have found out what was wrong.

EXAMPLE: Listening

"I'm through, Andy—done, finished! I've had it with this place! I quit!"

"Wow! What happened, Graham?"

"I don't even want to talk about it. I just want out!" shouted Andy.

"It must have been pretty bad."

"It was. No matter how hard you work around here, they never show you any respect. Never!"

"Did something go wrong with the new automated cataloging system you've been developing?" asked Graham.

"Not some thing—some *one*. Actually, several someones. You'd think I'd never installed a system in my life, from the way they talked to me."

"Mrs. Shields didn't like the modification?"

"She never saw it. I was trying to bring it up when the terminal died on me, and I couldn't bring it back. They started making comments, as if it were my fault and I didn't know what I was doing."

"It sounds like they were pretty rough on you."

"That's putting it mildly."

"It also sounds to me like you got pretty frustrated with the system yourself."

"I did. I'm so tired of these ancient terminals. They should have been turned in two years ago. Instead . . ."

(**WHAT IF** Andy had just taken Graham at his word when he said he didn't want to talk? What would have happened? How would Graham have felt an hour later?)

"Listening is very important," Fred continued, "and there's something else useful you can . . ."

There was a loud knock and the door opened. Reggie Rosenfeld stuck his head in and said, "You'll have to leave. We have the room reserved for the rest of the day."

"That's a fine kettle of fish," Paula responded. "Just where do you think we can go?"

"Well, the easiest thing would be just to move to the next chapter. It's empty."

"I guess we could—but what about all the stuff we've written on the blackboard? Do we have to copy it and write it up again?"

"No," Fred said emphatically. "This is a book and we can do anything we want. Let's just take the blackboard with us. . . ."

CHAPTER 12

Communicating, Part II

PHASE ONE MANAGEMENT	
Structuring	C
Selecting	O
Guiding	M
Correcting	M
Motivating	U
Delegating	N
Supporting	I
	C
	A
	T
	I
	N
	G

In this chapter, you'll find useful information on:

Giving and receiving feedback.

Being persuasive.

Nothing has changed much since the last chapter. Good communication skills are absolutely essential for developing successful workers.

THE DISCUSSION RESUMES

Giving Feedback

Fred hung the blackboard on the wall and closed the door behind the others. "As I was saying, there's something else useful you can do when you're listening, and it's one of my main concerns: feedback. If you reflect back to the speaker what you heard, you show that you're listening, *and* you give him a chance to correct you if you misunderstood. I don't think it's possible to be clear or to listen effectively without feedback."

"Will it surprise you if I agree with you completely?" Paula asked. "One of the big mistakes people make when they're trying to persuade others is talking most of the time. Nothing turns people off quicker than that. The worse thing is, you never know it . . . Well, actually you do know it—but not until later when you find out you screwed up."

Fred tapped Paula on the shoulder. "Right! The first time I heard about feedback, I realized I rarely used it. So, I set myself goals for more than a month to make sure I gave people feedback. I actually kept a record. For the first week, I did it at least five times a day. By the end of the month, I was up to 10 to 20 times a day. Boy, did that ever help! Now, it's the most natural thing in the world for me to do."

"I won't say 'Amen,'" Clarice told him, grinning, "because I don't want this to sound like a prayer meeting. But it's true. You know, an important part of feedback is remaining objective and not getting involved and judgmental. If you sound like you're accusing the other person of something when you give feedback, he'll have the opposite reaction from what you want."

"Yes," Helen agreed. "When you can give feedback objectively, you can give the people you work with useful responses. This is especially important when you have to provide correction to workers on their performance or conduct.

"Some of my workers have told me that I used to sound very judgmental when I talked with them about improving their performance. It's no wonder I didn't get anywhere! Now, I sit down and try to discuss their work with them objectively, as if we were talking about how to hang a picture or prune a tree. It works, too."

"Do you know why?" Paula jumped in. "When you use a judgmental approach, you sound as though you're attacking the *person*. When you remain objective, you can talk about what the individual *did*, not what he is. I think that's so important because feedback isn't judging or evaluating someone else. It's giving him useful information about how you see his ideas or his work or his behavior. You can be completely objective and still do it effectively."

EXAMPLE: Giving Feedback

"Bertha, you're just not applying yourself. I don't know what's the matter with you. Your work used to be so good, but now it's barely satisfactory. I don't think you care about things any more."
or
"Bertha, the quality of your work seems to be falling off. What's wrong?"

"Ms. Kersey, you're not being fair to me in the way you're assigning work."

"And I don't think you're being very fair to walk in here and accuse me of that. Is that how a good employee should behave?"

"Well, I hate to complain, but it's been bothering me. I really don't feel . . ."

"I'm sorry if you're bothered, but you'll just have to accept the fact that we're very busy right now."

"But . . ."
or
"Ms. Kersey, you're not being fair to me in the way you're assigning work."

"I'm sorry you feel that way. How am I being unfair?"

"I always get the jobs that require the most calculations. The others don't have to calculate nearly as much as I do."

"So you think that I'm assigning you the jobs with the most calculations because I'm unfair?"

"Yes—I don't know why else you'd do it. I hate to . . ."

(**WHAT IF** you used the second response to each pair of examples instead of the first? How do you think the worker would react? How would his reaction differ if you used the first?)

Dealing With Defensiveness

"You know, Paula, I'm getting a completely different picture of you from the one I had. You're not the glib salesman I thought you were.

Actually, I guess you're not a sales*man* at all." Everyone laughed with Helen at the way she accented the statement. "But I want to ask the group something: What do you do with someone who gets defensive when you give him feedback, and he reacts as though you're criticizing him?"

"That's a good question," Fred responded, "and I don't have a pat answer. But I can tell you some of the things I do:

First of all, it doesn't do you any good to attack the person. When someone gets defensive, it's very easy to start verbally beating him over the head. All that does, though, is make him even more defensive.

Second, if you can, ask the person to explain what he's reacting to. When someone is defensive, it's because he thinks you're attacking him in some way. If you can get the person to tell you why he feels like he's being attacked, you have a chance to reassure him and to communicate what you're trying to get across.

Third, if it's your boss or another manager who's getting defensive, you may have to back off and try again some other time. But keep doing the other things we've been talking about: Be open, honest, and clear; and listen responsively. When you act this way, most people will start to trust you. Then they'll be more open to what you have to say.

If it's a worker, you may want to back off for awhile, too. But there's one more thing involved in this case. A worker should understand that giving performance feedback is part of your job and that listening to it and using it is part of *his* job. It's part of being a successful worker—and it's almost impossible to be successful without it.

And that brings me to the last point. If you want people to accept feedback from you, you should ask them to give feedback to you— and ask them sincerely. Nothing's a one-way street. One of the luckiest things that can happen to you is to find someone who will tell you honestly how he thinks you're doing.

If you do find someone who'll give you objective feedback, great—but don't count on it. If the only way you can get feedback is by letting someone yell at you, then do it that way. The important thing is to look for the feedback, make it clear that you want it, and accept it.

"There, that's what I know about handling people who get defensive when they're given feedback."

"Would you agree with something?" Larry asked. "A person can accept feedback and use it without having to agree with it, can't he?"

"Certainly—and I'm glad you added that. Neither you nor a worker has to accept another's feedback uncritically, but you should listen to it. If you don't understand it, or it doesn't sound right, ask questions. Think about it. Accept it as useful information, then decide what use to make of it."

"May I give you an example?" Clarice asked. "Just yesterday, one of my people told me I wasn't being fair with her in the way I assigned work. I was really tempted to jump on her because she's not one of my best workers—but I didn't. It turned out that she was uncomfortable doing calculations. I took care of that, but I used her feedback in another way, too. What she said helped me realize that I haven't been paying enough attention to my group's training needs lately."

"That's a good example—thanks," Helen said. "Let me try to tie defensiveness to something we were talking about a bit earlier. Defensiveness is caused by fear. People get defensive when they think someone is attacking them or trying to take something away from them. As a manager, the more open you are, the easier you are to trust. I don't disagree with anything anyone has said, but in the long run the best way to deal with defensiveness is to be open and trustworthy."

EXAMPLE: Dealing with Defensiveness

"Dorothy, we need to talk about your production."

"Oh, has somebody been complaining to you that I'm not carrying my share of the load, Mrs. Washington?"

"Actually, no one needed to. I can tell from the production figures, which I'll be glad to show you if . . ."

"Don't bother. I *knew* you were going to hassle me."

"No, I don't want to hassle you at all—but we do need to talk about your output."

"Sure, and how many others have you talked to about their 'output'? I'll bet you haven't talked to anyone else!"

"It doesn't really matter, does it? What's important to us is *your* production."

"Okay, here it comes. Preach me the sermon."

"I don't have to . . . Wait a minute, Dorothy. What's really bothering you about all this?"

"*You're* bothering me, picking on me like this. You're just like the others. I can't do anything right!"

"I'm sorry to hear that. I think you can be a good worker. Does it seem to you that I don't?"

"You've been so hard on me lately. I think you believe I'm no good at all."

"I know it's painful to feel that way. Is that why you don't want to talk about your performance?"

"I . . . I'm afraid you're going to tell me you're going to fire me. . . ."*

(**WHAT IF** Helen had gotten angry when Dorothy got defensive? What would have happened to the discussion?)

*Many of the examples in this book are compressed in time. Most incidents in real life take longer to develop. That's particularly true of this one. Defensiveness is often a deep-seated personal characteristic that doesn't change in a few words or sentences. A manager would be very lucky to get an employee to talk about his real fears as quickly as the one in this example did.

That doesn't mean the example useless. If you with others with honesty and concern, it can—usually will—help them be less defensive. Just expect it to take longer than in the example.

Persuading

There was a pause. Paula broke it with, "Okay, we've covered the other communication skills. Is it all right if I talk about persuasion now?"

She looked around. Most of the others grinned at her, and they all nodded. "Good! I don't want to downplay anything anyone has said. I hope I've convinced you that I believe those skills are important, too. But now that I've said that, let me also say that no manager's communication skills are complete until he's a good persuader."

"Look how often you have to use persuasion: getting your people to put in overtime when they don't want to; convincing them to try a new method; persuading your boss to let you run things your way; trying to influence another manager to put your group at the top of his priority list for supplies or work. The list goes on and on—don't you agree?"

"Yes," Helen responded, "we really do have to be persuasive. Keep in mind, though, that if we have an effective, open relationship with our workgroups, we'll spend more time trying to solve problems with our workers and less time trying to persuade them to do what we want. The same thing applies when we have good relationships with other managers and bosses. Most of the times we need to use persuasion are those when we don't have a good relationship."

"Hmmm . . . Okay, I'll buy that," Paula said. "If I stop and think about it, that's one time when I have to use persuasion myself. There's another instance, too: when you want to make a quick decision and there's no time to work the situation through with everyone and develop a consensus. This is particularly true if the decision involves a significant change. To get the support you need in that kind of situation, you'd better be quite persuasive.

"I really do know that being open, communicating clearly, listening responsively, and using feedback are all part of being persuasive. But persuasion involves even more—can you agree with me on that?"

There was a pause, and then most of the group nodded. "Maybe we haven't paid enough attention to persuasion," Larry said. "What do you have to do to be persuasive?"

Paula smiled. "The very first thing is the one most people overlook: You have to *know your audience and what's important to them.* That applies whether you're working with an individual worker or dealing with a room full of executives. The more you know about your audience—how they think, how they feel, what they want—the more persuasive you can be. And, Larry, although you don't just do this by listening, listening responsively can be an important part of it."

Larry nodded.

Paula continued, "Knowing your audience isn't something you only do b*efore* you try to persuade them. You keep trying to understand them better by getting their reactions as you go along. You ask for feedback, you watch their body language—whatever clues you can get. If you don't, you have no idea how they're reacting; you can lose them completely and not realize it."

"You know I'm going to agree with you there," Fred said.

"I suspected it. Now, though, let's go to the second requirement: You've got to be able to *show your audience how what you want them to do will help them meet their important goals.* You want them to see that . . ."

Helen interrupted. "Paula, that sounds terribly manipulative to me. I'm not sure I could do it."

"I think you may be misunderstanding Paula here," Fred said to Helen. "When I was shopping for a television set a few weeks ago, I went to half a dozen places. The first five were all alike; the salespeople asked me what kind of set I wanted and how much I wanted to pay. Then they showed me everything they had anywhere close to that price range.

"The man at the last place I went to was different. He spent two or three minutes asking me just how I was going to use the set. Then he showed me three models. He explained the differences among them, told me how much each of them cost, and asked me what else he could tell me about them. You've probably guessed that that's where I bought my set. And I think that's the kind of persuading Paula is talking about—at least I hope so.

"It is, and thank you. What you've said ties right into the third thing you need to keep in mind: *the best persuasion is the selling that the other person does inside himself*. You give your audience all they need to know—and, let's be honest, you put the best face on it you can—then you let them take over. Pushing too hard is the worst thing you can do. As much as I believe in persuasion, I think high-pressure selling is the pits. I get my satisfaction from believing that I've done someone a service. By the way, that's exactly how I look at it when it's my own workgroup or another manager that I'm trying to influence."

"That sounds like 'persuading with integrity,'" Helen said. "I think I can agree with that."

"Me, too," Clarice added, "but let me add one other idea. I remember reading a long time ago that one of the best recruiting devices was a good reputation—and I think that's true of persuasion, too. *You influence people a lot more by what you are than what you say.* If they think you're a solid, trustworthy person on whom they can depend, they'll be a lot easier to persuade. If they think you're trying to put one over one them, you're doomed."

"Thank you," Paula said, "I really appreciate your adding that. In the long run, it's what we are that persuades people—or doesn't persuade them. That's what ties persuasion in with the other characteristics. Even in the most superficial relationships, where you have to depend on persuasiveness most heavily, the kind of person you are starts to show through. As the old saw puts it: 'What you are speaks so loudly that they can't hear what you say.'"

EXAMPLE: Persuading

"I stopped work early today," the unit manager began, "and called you together for a specific reason. Some of you are really against the idea of doing a just-in-time inventory system for the branch. I understand why you're concerned. I know you're all thinking about what happened in Building 3. I admit that was a mess but I've looked into it, and I don't think we have anything to worry about. They weren't ready to do the system, and we are.

"In fact, this could be a real opportunity for us. We've worked hard for the last year to get Division to recognize the good job we do. If we put in a just-in-time system and it works—and it will work, believe me—we'll show everybody just how good we are.

"I want you each to think about that. We'd be the first unit in the Division to implement just-in-time successfully. Ask yourself how it would feel to have people saying that about you.

"For some of you, it may boil down to this—and I'm asking you to trust me. I've looked the proposal over carefully, and I'm convinced we can make it work. I don't think I've ever let you down before, and I promise you I won't this time. . . ."

(**WHAT IF** the manager had more time available to deal with the idea of a just-in-time inventory system? What else might he have done to "sell" the idea?)

Some Tips

There was a long pause while everyone digested the discussion. Then Larry spoke. "Can I add one more thing? How you communicate makes a tremendous difference. When I think about all we've said, it really seems to me that the more informal the communication, the better. I know I prefer face-to-face discussions, like this one. Putting something in writing really inhibits me."

"I agree," Helen commented, "and there's one situation where I think this is especially true. All of us have to deal with the unpleasant aspects of our jobs—you know, giving performance appraisals to poor workers, correcting workers who don't want to be corrected, dealing with angry managers or customers. It's a tremendous temptation to duck the unpleasantness of a one-on-one and communicate in writing. I can tell you from hard experience, though, that's a poor way to operate."

"Yes, it is," Clarice replied, "and it's particularly a poor way to operate when you're dealing with a union. Just as there are all kinds of unions, there are all kinds of relationships between unions and management, and even the best of them can get tense. It's oh so easy to put everything in writing and 'let 'em do what they want with it'— but it doesn't work. It's amazing how much you can accomplish, even if the overall relationship is bad, if you're willing to deal honestly with the steward face-to-face."

"It is," Fred said, "but it takes time. If you think you have to be patient when you're getting workers to trust you, just try it with a suspicious union steward. I've been in my job over a year, and the steward is just now reaching the point where she'll come and talk to me instead of firing off a grievance. She wouldn't admit it, but it's already made life easier for both of us."

"Well, folks, it's been charming—but it's also been long. I need to get back to my office and take care of some things, and I expect you do, too." Paula looked around questioningly, and several of the others nodded.

"Can I suggest that we each write down the points that were most important to us? Then we can read them to each other and make any additions. When we're finished, we'll pass them along to whomever called this meeting in the first place."

"Good idea, Paula." Clarice got the pads and pencils from the center of the table, passed them around, and they all began writing.

When it looked like everyone was done, Paula spoke up again. "Let's go around the table, and each person will give . . ."

A QUICK SUMMARY

They did, and this is what they worked out:

1. *Being open and honest* is the first characteristic of an effective communicator.
   a. If a manager isn't open and honest, people waste time and energy trying to guess what's really happening.
   b. Effective management requires trust. People will trust those who are open and honest with them.

   c. Openness means two different things:
      1. The manager acts genuinely and doesn't play some kind of role.
      2. The manager is open to input from others. The goal is what's best, not what's "yours" or "mine."
   d. When there is a real give-and-take in the workgroup, people become more willing to change.

2. Communicating *clearly* is the next characteristic.
   a. When a worker doesn't do what was asked, it's probably because the manager wasn't clear.
   b. Nothing communicates better than clear, simple English. Jargon and "bureaucratese" are confusing to people who don't use them all the time.
   c. A manager should take steps to see that what he writes is clear.
      1. Compose out loud to see how things sound before writing them down.
      2. Test what's been written by showing it to an "average" reader and clarify anything that's misunderstood.
   d. Being clear and simple is a necessary part of being open and honest.

3. Listening *responsively* means a manager doesn't just listen but *shows* the other person that he's paying attention.
   a. A good listener is a *responsive* listener, not a passive one.
   b. A good listener leans forward, makes eye contact, gestures—whatever is needed to show that he is hearing the other person.
   c. A good listener asks questions, which helps him learn, and shows interest in the subject.

4. Using *feedback* is essential for successful communication.
   a. Without feedback, a manager never knows whether he is being heard accurately. Two people who think they're agreeing can have completely different ideas—and vice versa.
   b. A manager must know how to give feedback objectively, not judgmentally.
      1. Being objective is very important when a manager is providing correction to workers on their performance or conduct.

2. A manager who is judgmental sounds like he's attacking the person. The objective is to deal with what the individual does, not what he *is*.

c. Feedback is an excellent way for a manager to show he's really listening.

d. Even the most objective manager sometimes has to deal with *defensiveness*.

1. Attacking the person who's being defensive only makes him more defensive.

2. A person becomes defensive when he feels he's being attacked. When this happens, a manager should try to find out why the person feels that way.

3. A manager sometimes needs to back off when someone is being defensive and try again another time.

4. The best defense against defensiveness is to be open and honest, to communicate clearly, and to listen responsively. Most people will trust others who behave this way.

5. A worker should understand that giving performance feedback is part of a manager's job and listening to it is part of a worker's job.

e. A manager who expects to give feedback must learn to seek and accept it himself—in any form.

f. Accepting feedback doesn't necessarily mean agreeing with what's said, but it does mean listening carefully and using the information.

5. Being persuasive, while an effective trait when combined with the other communication skills, isn't a substitute for them.

a. Sometimes, though, a manager has to use persuasive skills—especially when there isn't time to develop open and trusting relationships or when he has to make a decision quickly but needs others' support.

b. The first requirement for being a persuasive manager is knowing the audience. This includes getting constant feedback in order to gauge the audience's reaction.

c. The second requirement is being able to show the audience how what the manager wants them to do will help them meet their important goals.

    d. The best persuasion is often the selling that goes on inside the other person.

    e. Most of the time, what persuades (or doesn't persuade) others is the credibility of the persuader.

6. General Thoughts

    a. Communication is most effective when it's face-to-face and informal.

    b. This is particularly true of unpleasant situations, which should always be handled face-to-face, if possible. The manager shouldn't hide behind the impersonality of a written communication.

    c. Communicating in person is also a good rule for dealing with union representatives. The more informal and open these contacts are, the more useful they will be for both parties.

"Wow," said Helen. "That was quite a morning's work!"

BACK TO THE SKILLS MAXIMIZATION MODEL

The previous nine chapters have dealt with the basic activities of Phase One Management and its basic skill—communication. Together, these activities and the skill of communicating make up the Phase One Management block of our skills maximization model. The model now looks as it is shown on the following page.

The next chapter will fill in one more block of the model—the fully successful workgroup.

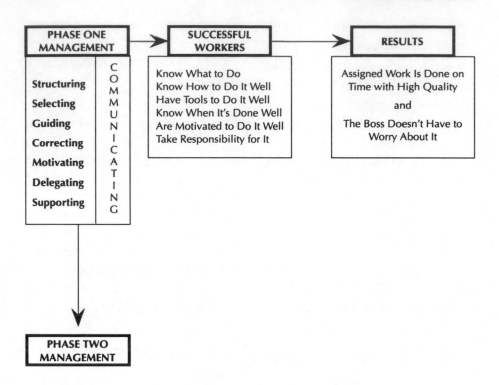

StretchMeter 9: COMMUNICATING

1. I am open and honest with my workgroup.

NEVER   1   2   3   4   5   6   7   8   **ALWAYS**

2. I state things clearly.

NEVER   1   2   3   4   5   6   7   8   **ALWAYS**

3. I listen responsively to others.

NEVER   1   2   3   4   5   6   7   8   **ALWAYS**

4. I give and receive feedback.

NEVER   1   2   3   4   5   6   7   8   **ALWAYS**

5. I am persuasive.

NEVER   1   2   3   4   5   6   7   8   **ALWAYS**

6. I prefer to communicate face-to-face in difficult situations.

NEVER   1   2   3   4   5   6   7   8   **ALWAYS**

Communicating ASAP

1. Openness and honesty are often difficult, but they're the basis of successful communication. If you and your workgroup aren't used to interacting on that basis, start slowly. Here's one way to begin: Select a problem the group needs to work out (but not a major one). Perhaps it's something you've been trying to get them to do without telling them why, or it's a change that's coming that you haven't told them about yet. Whatever it is, call them together and tell them that you want to have more openness in the group. Then give them the information you've been holding back. If you can get reactions to it, so much the better. If you can't (and you probably can't at this stage), don't give up. Continue being open and asking for responses. After a while, the openness will become mutual.

2. Using clear and simple language isn't easy; most organizations encourage the reverse. The best place to start is with the two techniques mentioned in Chapter 11. First, say out loud what you want to write before you write it. Don't write it down until it *sounds* clear to you. Second, try out what you want to say (both written and spoken) on someone who's typical of your audience. Then ask him to paraphrase what you've said back to you. If he doesn't understand it, go back to the old drawing board.

3. Remember, effective listening means not only listening carefully but showing the other person that you're listening. Fortunately, it's an easy skill to practice—start today. At least five times a day for two weeks, listen responsively. Do it in a casual conversation at break or over lunch, when you're hearing a complaint, while getting directions from your boss—whenever. Spend at least 80 percent of that time listening. Use body language, short comments, and questions to show the person who's talking that you're listening. When the two weeks are over— do it for the rest of your life.

4. Communicating clearly, listening responsively, and using feedback can't be separated. If you're not comfortable using feedback, try ASAP 3—but concentrate on feedback. Questions can be part of it: "Do you mean that . . . ?" So can statements like "It sounds to me like what you're saying is . . ." and "Let me make sure I understand you here. As you see it, . . ." When

you're comfortable doing that, you can move on to feedback about behavior and performance. ("This is how what you did this morning struck me. . . .")

5. The best way to begin being persuasive is to understand your audience. They'll hear only what they *can* hear, so you need to think about what they can hear. Answer for yourself a few general questions: How old are they? How well educated are they? How much do they know about the subject? You also need to answer specific questions, such as "Has something happened to them to make them like (or dislike) what I'm proposing?" When you're comfortable doing this, move on to the next step (identifying what's important to them), and then the next, and the next.

6. It's hard to communicate face-to-face when things are tense—but that's when it's needed most. The way to get started is similar to that for ASAP 1: Pick one of your easier problems and talk to the person involved. *Don't* expect that he will respond positively (though he may). If things stay tense, they stay tense. Don't get emotionally involved; stay cool and stay with the problem. This type of communicating takes some getting used to, but it pays immense dividends.

CHAPTER 13

Creating Successful Teams

SUCCESSFUL WORKGROUP
Transformed into a Self-Managing Team

In this chapter, you'll find useful information about:

The first steps required to transform a fully successful workgroup into a self-managing team.

When a manager develops a successful workgroup, it's an easy step for him to help them transform into a self-managing team—giving him time to concentrate on Phase Two Management and increase his value to the organization.

A QUICK INTRODUCTION TO SELF-MANAGEMENT

"Damn!" Eduardo Navarro exclaimed, dropping heavily into the chair across from Chuck Weldon. "They've done it again!"

Chuck grinned. If there was a person who could find the cloud behind every silver lining, it was Ed. "What is it this time?"

"You haven't heard? Now we're going to start using self-managing teams. You and I are going to be as extinct as the dodo this time next year."

Chuck's grin vanished and he leaned forward. "They're finally getting the message. Thank heavens."

"Thank heavens?? We're going to lose our jobs, and you say 'Thank heavens'?!"

"Calm down, Ed. Sure, some of the people who are first-level managers or so will have to do something else. But they're still going to need some of us; we'll just be doing different things." He relaxed and leaned back. "Actually, my workgroup is almost a self-managing team now. Let me see if I can show you."

The two of them walked down the hall and into Chuck's area. Beverley Stallings paused to let them by, then walked quickly to Eleanor Watkins's cubicle.

Chuck grabbed Ed's arm. "Let's watch this," he said. They both stopped.

"Hey, El, got a minute?"

Eleanor looked up to see Beverley. "What's up, Bev?"

"Mitzi and Lee have run into a snag with the mod they're working on. I thought maybe we could help them."

"Sure I've got a headache from staring at these charts, anyway."

Eleanor and Beverley walked across the aisle to Mitzi's cubicle. She and Lee were frowning at a printout, tracing an invisible flow from page to page.

"Oh, hi," Mitzi said. "I know you're both busy, but if you could give us a hand, it would sure be great. Somehow or another, this thing gets lost in never-never land. Lee's been helping me for an hour but, frankly, neither of us has a clue."

Beverley and Eleanor bent over the printout. Everyone was quiet for a moment. "I'll bet *that's* it," Beverley said. She pointed at a line of code, then back up to a statement two pages earlier.

"Yep, I think you've got it. Mitzi, do you and Lee see what happened here?" For the next few minutes, she and Eleanor explained the problem, until both Mitzi and Lee were nodding vigorously.

"Listen, I have a thought," Eleanor said. "Angel is absolutely brilliant at loops. There are a couple of things I've been wanting to ask him, and I think he could show you several better ways to handle that particular step. Let's see if he's avaiable."

"Not right now," Angel said as the four of them squeezed into his small office. "We owe the interface design to Marketing this afternoon, and I need another couple of hours before it's done. Tell you what, though: Lee, if you and Mitzi will help me with this for half an hour, I'll meet the four of you for coffee in the conference room at 3:30, and we can end up the day with our own symposium."

Chuck grinned broadly and looked at Ed.

"Do you just let them run around like that?" Ed asked, wrinkling his brows.

"They're not 'running around'; they're managing themselves and doing a really good job at it. And just in case you don't believe me, my two teams have had the highest overall productivity in the division for four months now."

EXAMPLE: How a Workgroup Becomes Self-Managing

When Mariam Soleau asked Chuck how he got his workgroup to be self-managing, this is what he said:

"I've never liked looking over people's shoulders all the time to make sure they were working and doing what they were supposed to do. I know that my kids don't need that kind of supervision, and I figured that if they didn't, the adults in my workgroup didn't. I'd read a little about self-managing teams, so I read a little more and then started thinking about how I could help my people be self-managing.

"I realized that I had done a good job of delegating to them, but I'd delegated to them as individuals. So I asked myself how I could help them be more of a team.

"Eleanor and Angel are my two senior programmers, so I started with them. We began holding meetings every few days to talk about the section, look at problems, try to do a little planning— that sort of thing. While we did this, it gave me a chance to help them understand what Phase One Managing involves. Angel really had a hard time with the idea that the job of a manager is to make his people successful, but he came around.

"When I thought they had picked up the basics, I gave each one of them a team assignment. Everybody wanted the office to be more open, so Angel headed a team that worked on redesigning the space. Bev is pretty social, so she ended up leading a team to plan the Christmas party (a lot harder job than you might think, by the way). When their teams had come up with their recommendations, they had to present them to the rest of the section, and we made the decisions as a group.

"Fortunately, both of the teams did a great job. Frankly, they surprised me. So I started assigning projects by team; sometimes just two or three people would make up the team, sometimes the whole workgroup. I sat in with them occasionally, to make sure they were doing what they needed to do—but they're a good group and I did less and less of that.

"Now, they report to me on a regular schedule on how the projects are coming, and they ask me for help if they think they need it. Otherwise, I don't interfere. It's not perfect, but it's working really well."

(**WHAT IF** Chuck continued to practice Phase One Management in this situation? What might happen?)

"I just don't understand something," Ed said. "You and I have both studied Phase One Management; we both agree it's necessary—and now you're not doing it."

"Not quite," said Chuck. "I still do some, though a little less every day. The reason I don't need to do some functions is that the team does them. In fact, *when we say a team is self-managing, we mean specifically that the team takes over most or all of the Phase One Management functions.* It structures itself, selects its members, guides and corrects them as necessary, motivates them, delegates tasks among team members, supports team members, and communicates within the team and with other teams and (often) higher levels. It also assures that its assigned work is done on time with high quality—and that higher management seldom if ever has to worry about its performance.

"When a manager gets good at Phase One Management, he starts to have time for Phase Two Management but he doesn't really have the time he needs for it until his team learns Phase One Management and performs it for themselves."

THE ADVANTAGES OF SELF-MANAGING TEAMS

Ed looked puzzled as he walked away down the hall to his own section. As Chuck walked back to his office, he mentally reviewed the advantages of self-managing teams.

He was convinced that self-management was the most effective form of management there is. The people in his workgroup understood each other and knew how to make the most of each other's strengths. Once he'd made clear to them what needed to be done and when, he could leave most of the work to them.

And because his group was a team it was very stable and able to "roll with the punches." When something came up, they could deal with it themselves—they didn't have to wait for him to tell them what to do. When someone in the group was having problems, the others were there to help him.

(He remembered with a grin when Beverley was going through her very messy divorce. She started drinking heavily, and it began to affect her work. He was psyching himself up to talk to her about it and asked Eleanor for suggestions. "Don't fret it, boss," Eleanor had said; "we'll take care of this." The next afternoon, the whole group left together. Chuck had no idea what happened, but Beverley's drinking problem was gone the next day.)

He was also continually surprised at the quality of their ideas. Angel and Eleanor were the most creative of the group, but they seemed able to draw unexpected ideas from the others. Even Lee, who had been with the group less than six months, was coming up with valuable ideas.

One result of all this was his low loss rate, which every other manager in data processing envied. He knew that Bev and Angel had been contacted again and again. The first time, Bev had said "yes" and had gone to work for an insurance company across town. Two weeks later, she called and asked if she could have her old job back.

"Sure," he had said, "but why? I can't pay you what they're paying."

"I never thought I'd say this to another human being, Chuck, but money just isn't that important. This place is dog-eat-dog. Yesterday, I tried to get one of the analysts to explain the claims system to me. He told me that was what manuals were for. That was the last straw. I want back!"

There is one last benefit, he thought, one that paid off for both the organization and for him. Since he didn't have to spend his time managing the team's day-to-day work, he was free to build up his influence in the organization. He had time to work with other managers, both customers and suppliers, and to build up strong relationships with them. As much as he liked doing this, though, he was even beginning to turn some of it over to his team.

HOW TO DEVELOP A FULLY SUCCESSFUL WORKGROUP

Chuck had just gotten started on some reports when Matt Chekhov, the newest manager in the Systems & Programs division, walked in. "Chuck, do you have a moment I could ask you a few questions?"

Chuck nodded, so Matt walked in and sat down.

"I've read about self-managing teams, just like you have. I really would like to get my people working together that way. But no matter how much I suggest that they work together on things, it doesn't seem to make much difference. What am I doing wrong?"

What Makes an Effective Team?

"Well," Chuck said, "there are lots of factors, really. If you want, maybe we can stroll over to the next chapter later this afternoon; most of the factors are covered there. But I can tell you right now about the most important one, the one so many companies and managers overlook. If you want an effective team, it has to have a clear goal, one that won't get done unless the team does it. And every member of the team has to believe that the goal is important and be willing to work toward it. Having a goal like this will do more to get them to work together than all the 'motivational' talks you and I could make in a year.

"Now, let me tell you a secret about these goals. Teams work best when they work with a complete process or project, not just a fragment of it. And they work best when they are working for one customer or group of similar customers. That's the quickest way for them to develop what the books call 'ownership' of their work."

EXAMPLE: Effective Team Goals

Chuck's section is responsible for providing program support for the Administrative Department of his company. The support ranges anywhere from fixing a small glitch or making a small modification in a running program to designing new programs that take months to complete.

At first, Chuck assigned work strictly on experience and individual programmer's skills. Less experienced programmers got very small projects or small parts of larger projects. Angel and Bev got the really tough assignments, and because Angel really liked financial systems he usually got that work, while Bev got the more administrative work.

When Chuck talked with the section's customers, though, he found that they didn't really know who was working on specific projects or whom to call if they had questions. Chuck thought about that and decided that teams were the best way to fix it. He had already started using Bev and Angel as team leaders, so he talked with them and they decided to make each team responsible for a specific group of customers. Angel took Budget, Finance, and Accounting, while Bev got Human Resources, Purchasing, Supply, and Reproduction Services.

That started working more effectively, since Angel and Bev now felt responsible for their specific customers, while the customers knew whom they could talk with about any of their projects. But there was still a problem. If Bev gave a small project to Mitzi and the customer had a question, he would ask Bev, who would ask Mitzi, who would tell her so she could answer the customer. After about the third of these, Bev suggested at one of their meetings that when they gave projects to specific programmers or small teams, that programmer or team should deal directly with the customer.

The three of them discussed the idea at some length, then decided to try it. Things were a little shaky at first, but then started to come together. The programmers were happier, their customers were happier, and—most of all—the quality of the section's service to its customers went up.

"If you want good work and high morale," Chuck said from then on, "give everyone a specific customer and make him responsible for satisfying that customer. You'll be amazed what a difference it makes!"

(**WHY** do you think it makes so much difference to a worker to know exactly who his customer is? Think of as many reasons as you can.)

How Teams Can Go Wrong

"That makes good sense," Matt said,"and I already have some ideas on how to do it in my own section. Let me change the subject, though, and ask you about something else. You make it sound like teams and teamwork are good no matter what—but that just doesn't square with what I've seen in this and other places I've worked."

Chuck grinned. "Right on. I've seen just as many teams struggling or even just plain failing as you have. I don't know all of the reasons, but there are five of them that seem pretty clear:

1. Every member of the team has to believe that the team's goal is *worthwhile*. If somebody thinks it doesn't really need to be done, or it's not worth his time, he's not going to commit himself to doing it. I remember that first team I set up to plan the Christmas party. I knew they were having trouble, but I didn't know why until I found out that Walter didn't believe the office ought to sponsor parties. I switched him to the other team because he did care about the office and things improved in a hurry.

2. I also learned the hard way that when you set up a team every member of it should be neces*sary*. At first, I'd put someone on a team because he didn't have anything to do or because I wanted him to learn some particular technique. Stop and think what that does: The team has to spend time and energy trying to find a job for him, while he feels frustrated because he's not adding anything. You can guess that I stopped that in a hurry.

3. It also disrupts a team if you put an *individualist* on it who just doesn't want to work with other people. I'm lucky, I don't have anyone like that. But it was close. For a long time, Raye really just wanted to go into a corner with her own project and be left alone. I thought I was going to have to let her work by herself, but several of the other programmers managed to persuade her to give teaming a try. She's still very much the individualist, but she's made her peace with the team, and she works well as a team member. When this happens, it's great. When it doesn't, you hurt both the team and the individual by trying to make him work in a way he's not comfortable with—and you or the organiza-

tion needs to find an individual job for the person and let him do it.

4. One of the big problems, and one that bothers me constantly, is the question of *rewards or incentives* for teams. We have an individual reward system, but what matters for team success is the whole team, not an individual star. I've tried and tried to get Human Resources to come up with a team award of some kind, but they just haven't done it. We do give some individual rewards, or at least the teams do. Mostly, though, we want the entire team to be rewarded when it succeeds—but we just haven't come up with a good way to do this so far. The best we can do is to hold a 'miniparty' in the office every time a team finishes a project on time and makes its customer happy. We sure would like to see the system changed, though.

5. The last problem has probably wrecked more teaming programs than anything else I've seen: *using teams inappropriately.* The best way to look at a team is as a 'group of people who need each other to succeed.* If you're serious about this, you'll look carefully at the work to be done. If one person can accomplish it, give it to him and get on to the next project. If it really does require more than one person to get done, pick just those workers you need for the team and give them the job. Remember, no matter how popular teams are, when an individual can do the work by himself, he will almost always do it better and faster than a team can. In fact, effective teams often dole out responsibilities to individuals or subteams just because of this.

EXAMPLE: How to Do Teaming Wrong

"Gentlemen, and you ladies, too, we have decided to adopt self-managing teams in the company to help us be more competitive.

*This is based on the definition used by Arie de Geus of Shell Oil Company, as quoted in Peter Senge's *The Fifth Discipline* (New York: Doubleday Currency, 1990), page 236. In de Geus's definition, teams are individuals who need each other to *act*. I prefer to look at the results—success—rather than the actions that get the results.

"Now we want each one of you managers to divide your workgroups up into teams. Our consultant says that teams shouldn't be larger than 10 people, so go by that. And make sure that everyone in the group is on a team; we want 100 percent participation.

"I do have to caution you not to overboard. This company was built by strong individuals, and we want to make sure that we don't fall for 'groupthink.' Maybe later on we'll look into incentives for teams, but for now I want you to keep your eyes on your best performers and make sure they get recognized even if their team isn't the best.

"I know many of you are disappointed with what happened to Total Quality Management, but I want to assure you that we are absolutely committed to effective teams. We're going to give you two weeks to get ready, and then every two weeks after that you're going to report to Human Resources the number of teams you have and the number of projects assigned to them.

"Any questions?"

A QUICK SUMMARY

1. Effective managers can develop their workgroups into largely self-managing teams; they don't need to wait for an organizational program or extensive training.
2. Self-management is the most effective form of management there is.
3. Effectively self-managing teams are very stable and able to "roll with the punches."
4. Effectively self-managing teams produce high quality ideas.
5. Effectively self-managing teams have low loss rates, particularly when the (internal and external) organizations that compete for their members use traditional boss-led work groups.
6. Effectively self-managing teams share common goals, ones that each member believes are worthwhile.
7. Self-managing teams are most apt to succeed when they are responsible for a single process and/or for serving a single customer or group of customers.
8. When a manager or an organization rushes into teams without care-

ful planning, the team strategy often fails. Five of the most important causes of the failure are:

   a. The team as a whole or members on it don't believe that the team goal is worthwhile.

   b. The team doesn't need every member. Members get assigned to teams just to give them something to do or to let them learn something.

   c. Individuals who prefer to work alone are forced to work as part of a team.

   d. Managers continue to give rewards to individual performers, not to teams.

   e. And teams are used even when work could be done better by individual performers or traditional workgroups.

9. Self-managing teams give their managers more time for Phase Two Management, which is more useful both to them and to their organizations.

StretchMeter 10: SUCCESSFUL SELF-MANAGING TEAMS

1. I am developing my workgroup into an effective team.

NEVER   1   2   3   4   5   6   7   8   ALWAYS

2. My workgroup is self-managing.

NEVER   1   2   3   4   5   6   7   8   ALWAYS

3. All team members share common goals that they believe are worthwhile.

NEVER   1   2   3   4   5   6   7   8   ALWAYS

4. Each team is responsible for a single process and/or serves a single customer or group of customers.

NEVER   1   2   3   4   5   6   7   8   ALWAYS

5. I'm careful to set up teams so that each member is needed.

NEVER   1   2   3   4   5   6   7   8   ALWAYS

6. I see that workers aren't forced to work on teams unless they want to.

NEVER   1   2   3   4   5   6   7   8   ALWAYS

7. I reward my workers for working together as a team.

NEVER   1   2   3   4   5   6   7   8   ALWAYS

8. I have time for Phase Two Management.

NEVER   1   2   3   4   5   6   7   8   ALWAYS

Successful Self-Managing Teams ASAP

1. If you're not trying to develop your workgroup into one or more teams, you're missing out on tremendous potential. If you're working to make your workers successful and practicing what you read in the first 12 chapters, you're well on your way. Look again at what Chuck did to develop his workgroup and pick an action that you can begin implementing now.

2. A team can perform most effectively if it has learned to be self-managing. Everything in the ASAP 1 applies here. If you're dubious about what you do as a manager if your team manages itself, read Chapters 16 and 17 on Phase Two Management and then come back to this point.

3. You can't make the members of your team share common goals, but you can work with them to develop them. This is your function as a leader helping the team set goals to which everyone can commit themselves. If you haven't been doing that, *now* is the time to start. Within the next week, work with your workgroup—whether they're a team yet or not—to develop at least one goal that everyone can support. Then see that the group keeps its eyes focused on the goal. *No matter what your situation is, this is one of the most effective steps you can take to bring your workgroup together and produce high performance.*

4. If your workgroup is responsible only for a fragment of a process or if they don't deal with a clear group of customers, you need to attack this problem at once. Sketch out different kinds of organization you might use to remedy the problem. Concentrate on finding a process to manage that serves a clear customer or group of customers. Get support higher up the line to change the process or customers if you have to. But do it.

5. If you've fallen into the habit of putting individuals on teams just to have something to do with them, you need to start finding an alternative now. They're interfering with the team's performance. Find them something to do; if possible, put them on a team where they have a clear contribution to make. If not, find them individual work in your organization or another. But put them where they can contribute, and insist that they do so.

6. Don't try to make team players out of committed individualists. Give them the chance to be on a team. Do even more—
   encourage them to be on a team. But if they really want to work
   alone, do your best to find them jobs. If you don't have individual work, try to find another workgroup that does. But do
   something; forcing individualists to work on teams is disrup-
   tive to the teams and frustrates the individualists.

7. Rewarding your workers for producing results as a team is
   something you can start right now. Much of what you need is
   in the chapter on Motivating (Chapter 8). Begin right now to
   make it clear that you want them to work together—and that
   cooperation will be rewarded. Watch carefully for cooperation.
   When you find it, notice it. Reward it, even if it's just a verbal
   pat on the back. If the cooperation really helps accomplish
   something, reward it boldly. And keep rewarding it. Try to
   persuade your organization to establish team rewards, but don't
   wait for them to do it.

8. Having time for Phase Two Management is an outgrowth both
   of successful Phase One Management and of successfully developing teams. If you've done Phase One Management right,
   you now have the time for Phase Two. If not, look at this chapter and the ones before it, decide what you need to do, and do
   it.

CHAPTER 14

Developing Successful Teams

SUCCESSFUL WORKGROUP
Transformed into a Self-Managing Team

In this chapter, you'll find useful information about:

> The key factors you need to consider to develop an effective self-managing team.

Like individuals, when self-managing teams begin, they are inexperienced and immature. As they acquire experience, they mature and become effective. This chapter explains the basic ingredients in this process.

On his way in to work, Chuck bumped into Freda Wexler, the chief of the Telecommunications Branch.

"Hey, where were you yesterday?" she asked as he opened the door for her. "You certainly weren't at the teams workshop that the department held."

"Nah, we had an important project that I had to coordinate." (That was true, but it wasn't the reason. Chuck really thought he knew most of what he needed to know about teams. Besides, while he wouldn't admit it, he was irritated because the department paid no attention to him—and he was the one who had been developing self-managing teams for over a year.)

"I think you would have gotten something from it. You probably know most of this stuff, but the way Dr. Hume presented it tied a lot of things together for me."

Chuck perked up. "You think you really got enough that I ought to hear about it?"

"Yeah, I do."

"OK. Will you be available if I drop by your office at about ten?"

"Sure"

THE IMPORTANCE OF THE RIGHT MISSION AND TECHNOLOGY

Chuck showed up promptly at ten. Freda was sitting at her work table, several papers scattered in front of her. She motioned Chuck to sit down across from her, then spun one of the papers around so he could read it. It had a chart on it:

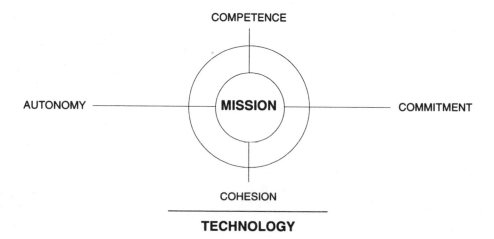

"Sure looks interesting," Chuck said after a moment, "but just what does it mean?"

"It says that a successful team:

1. Has a clear mission,
2. Is supported by the right technology, and
3. Balances commitment, cohesion, autonomy, and competence in its everyday functioning."

"If *mission* is about the same thing as *goals*, I understand that." (Freda nodded, so Chuck went on.) "I'm not real sure what you mean by *right technology*, though."

"Actually, that's an easy one. You and I both know that many managers think that, if they just automate something, everything will be okay." (Chuck nodded.) "Well, technology *is* important, but only if you use it in the right way to support the mission of the team. Just think how hard you've been working to get funds for a Computer-Aided Software Engineering system."

"Okay, I get that," Chuck answered thoughtfully. "We're at least 20 percent less productive than we'd be with a good CASE system—our old mainframe system hurts as much as it helps."

EXAMPLE: Using the Right Technology

Freda knew firsthand about the need for the right technology. As the company had grown, it had opened or acquired operations in seven different states. The job of Freda's branch was to tie them all together. They did the job well, but only because they had the technology they needed.

The systems, for instance, were reliable but very complex. It used to be that the technicians in the branch had to carry stacks of technical manuals with them whenever they went out to fix a problem. About a year before, though, their supplier started putting the manual on a CD-ROM.* That let the branch put a CD-

---

*Just in case you're not up on all the latest jargon, a CD-ROM is the computer version of a compact disk. It can store music, but more often it stores text, diagrams, pictures, even video. It can be plugged into a computer just like a hard disk. What makes it so valuable, though, is that each disk can store the equivalent of about 250 novels, or 100 million words.

ROM reader in each of their technicians' computers and replace half a dozen 3-inch-thick manuals with two CD-ROMs.

Of course, the technicians used fax machines and e-mail; almost everyone in the company did that. But none of that, even the CD-ROMs, helped with one of their major problems: Almost a third of their calls which each cost several hundred to several thousand dollars to make were to fix relatively routine problems. Their field operations were neither dumb nor lazy, but they seldom had anyone on their staff with the background to understand and fix the problem.

One of the senior technicians got the idea to develop a small expert system that would ask questions and then suggest to the field offices what the problem likely was. Most of the time, they could fix it themselves. When they couldn't, the technician could either explain the fix to them or take care of it in one short visit.

They got the software package and developed the expert system, which worked just like they hoped. In fact, it was so successful that the technician was promoted to a position writing similar expert systems for other parts of the company (about which Freda had definitely mixed feelings).

(Don't think, though, that right technology means "high-tech." It doesn't, and it doesn't mean focusing on the technology. It means *focusing on the team and its mission* and using the technology that best supports both the team and the mission. For instance, the workers and managers at the Saturn automobile plant in Spring Hill, Tennessee, decided early on not to adopt a high-tech approach—yet their self-managing teams produce one of the highest quality cars in the world. It's not the technology—it's the fit between the mission, the team, and the technology.)

(**WHAT IF** the technicians hadn't developed the expert system but had started tallying up the most common causes of the breakdowns and writing short guides to each cause?)

Chuck looked back at the diagram. "Okay, mission and technology seem clear enough. Now, what about commitment, cohesion, autonomy, and competence? And what do you mean when you talk about balancing them?"

WHAT COMMITMENT MEANS

"Dr. Hume called those four terms the team's 'dimensions of maturity.' What he meant by that, I think, is that they are the four areas in which teams grow and develop. In that sense, teams are like people; they start out immature and inexperienced and grow to be mature and competent. And, like people, it's important that they mature in a balanced way. We all know kids that are great at athletics or music but can't really relate to other kids. Well, unless they stay in balance, teams can end up like that, too."

"I probably could provide your Dr. Hume with some stories on that point," Chuck grinned. "Anyway, go on. Tell me about *commitment*."

"The way we used to run around here, and the way a lot of the company still runs, you didn't hear much about commitment except in motivational sessions. We didn't really expect workers to be committed to what they were doing. That's why we needed first-level managers, to see that workers who aren't really committed do what they're supposed to do.

"You and I both know that won't work if you're going to have self-managing individuals or teams. Workers just won't consistently perform at a high level because someone else is pushing at them. Let's be honest—neither will managers. To get the kind of performance that justifies self-managing teams, we have to have commitment, and not just a general commitment, but the personal commitment of each team member to the team's mission."

"I certainly agree with that. I also think I understand how to get that kind of commitment, but I'm curious what our visiting expert had to say about it."

"I think you do understand," Freda said, putting down her coffee cup. "Just for the record, though, she said that committed performance depends on doing challenging work, with significant autonomy, in a supportive work environment."

"Okay, I see that autonomy is on the diagram. But what about challenging work and a supportive work environment?"

"They're no real surprise. They just mean that the work itself is interesting and that individuals and teams are expected to learn from their mistakes but aren't chewed out because they make them. And an effective self-managing team is an extremely supportive environment, as you might expect."

EXAMPLE: Challenging Work in a Supportive Work Environment

Neither Chuck nor Freda knew Freddy Gomez, the chief of the Voucher Processing Branch, but they would have appreciated some of the changes he had made in the branch.

The branch had to process each traveler's vouchers before he could get reimbursed for travel. This made them very important to their customers (the travelers), who wanted their vouchers processed quickly and without errors.

Until Freddy got there, the branch never even came close. What he found was that one section logged in the vouchers and examined them for completeness. Then they sent them to the review section, which examined them for obvious errors. If they were error-free, they were sent to another section to do the computations, and then on to their final stop where they were entered into the computer for payment. If there were errors, the review section marked the errors and returned them to the travelers for correction.

Freddy saw quickly that none of the clerks did more than a fragment of the whole process. This meant the work was very boring and that no one ever had any real customers. It took him a while, but he got the branch reorganized into four teams. Each team processed the vouchers from a small group of organizations. This means that each team had a clear set of customers. Furthermore, because they were working in teams, team members could work at all of the different jobs. This made the work much more challenging for everyone; in fact, the tardiness problem Freddy had inherited almost entirely disappeared.

The teams not only provided challenging work, they supported all of the team members in doing it. They could fill in for one another and help train each other—and when a team member had a problem they could all pitch in and help. With the new organization, productivity went up. Just as important, the vouchers were processed much more rapidly, with very few errors—with so few errors that a team could contact a traveler who made an error and resolve it quickly over the phone. As a result, complaints from customers dropped off to almost nothing.

(**WHAT IF** Freddy couldn't have reorganized? What else could he have done to improve performance?)

WHY A TEAM NEEDS COHESION

Chuck nodded, then looked back at the diagram. "The next dimension is *cohesion*," he said. "Tell me about that."

"I expect we've both seen its good side and its bad side. The more cohesive a team is, the more closely its members work with each other and the more they think of themselves as a team, rather than just a collection of individual performers.

"I heard about a good example of that just the other day. Marsha Winfree has a team that handles receivables, and it really blew one of the discounts. Cost the company several hundred dollars. She wanted to deal with whoever did it, but the team insisted that the team as a whole was responsible—and it just wouldn't tell her who the individual was. She finally blew off steam at the team leader and let the situation be."

"Yeah, I get frustrated with each of my teams every once in a while because they act the same way. But when I see how effectively they work together, I wouldn't want them to be otherwise. A team just has to be cohesive to function. And the only way that can happen is for it to work together for a while."

"Yes and no. Cohesion happens when the individuals work together and get to know each other and what to expect from each other. The heart of cohesion, though, is trust. According to Dr. Hume, that's what every good team-building workshop is about—helping the team members to develop trust in each other.

EXAMPLE: A Quick Look at a Cohesive Team

"So you're just not going to tell me who blew the payment on the Augsberg account?"

"Marsha, I already told you the team blew it. We did it, and we take full responsibility for it."

"Well, I see there's no point in trying to talk with any of you any further. I'll leave it alone this time, but you'd better not let it happen again." Marsha glowered at Tom for a moment, then turned and walked away.

A few minutes later, at a team meeting, Tom asked, "Adele, isn't that one of your accounts?"

Adele answered, "Yes, but . . . ."

Sha-Ron interrupted. "Tom, it wasn't her fault. When she went on vacation last week, I told her I'd work her accounts for her. I guess I just plain skipped that line in the printout or something. Anyhow, when she got back yesterday, she caught it and made the payment right away."

"I really got mad at first," Adele said. "Sha-Ron will tell you I almost didn't speak to her yesterday after I found out. But then I got to thinking: Augsberg has a funny way of stating their discounts, and I expect that Sha-Ron has never run into anything like it. I'm going to get with her when we finish the meeting and go over it with her again. And, Sha-Ron, I want you to handle my accounts for me week after next while I'm away for training. This time," she pointed her finger at Sha-Ron, imitating an old-line manager they all knew, "I expect absolute perfection."

(**WHAT IF** Tom had told Marsha that Sha-Ron had made the mistake? How would that have affected the team?)

WHAT AUTONOMY REALLY MEANS

"Okay, that helps. I know all about the next one, autonomy. I've been telling Ryan for months that if he'd give me the freedom to do things my way, I could increase productivity even more. I think every one of us wants this freedom."

"We do, but there's really more to it than that. Dr. Hume was very clear that *autonomy* means the team has control over the factors that will make or break its success. It means that they can do things their own way, sure. But it also means that they're not at the mercy of another unit they can't control or of an automated system that isn't reliable. In other words, it involves more than just being able to do things your own way. Does that make sense?"

"Sure does," Chuck said, smiling ruefully. "Just last week, Bev's team missed a deadline because they were running a little late with their test and right in the middle of the test, Operations shut the system down for updating. It broke their string of on-time, in-budget products, and boy were they mad!"

"No wonder! Dr. Hume really stressed analyzing the work situation up front to identify the barriers to team success and then doing something about them."

EXAMPLE: Planning for Autonomy

"Marie, we're all set to take over as a self-managing team next week, with one exception."

Marie Glover put down her pen and looked up at Denzel Smith. "Okay—shoot."

"We've just got to find some alternative to your reviewing every one of our products. With your schedule, it takes you anywhere from hours to days to do a review—and that could make us blow a deadline."

"Denzel, I appreciate your concern, but the department expects me to review all of our reports before they go out."

"I know that's how we've done it before, but things are supposed to be different now. Every member of the team had the short consulting workshop week before last, and we've had two meetings about negotiating out what our customers want. We've talked to each customer and signed a brief memorandum of agreement on what we expect from each other. We're ready to go, if you'll just let us."

Marie rolled the pen in her fingers. "And just what do you think I should do?"

"Got that one covered. We think we ought to meet with you as a team at least once a week—more often if you want—and bring you up to date on each project. We've worked out an evaluation form to send with each report; it comes back to us, but we'll send you a copy as soon as we get it. Don't you think that ought to be enough for now?"

Marie grinned. "Okay, I'll try it for 90 days. But you guys had better not let me down or all of us will be named 'mud.' "

"Don't give it a second thought," Denzel said as he walked out. "In 90 days, we'll be the King—and you'll be the Queen—of the Block."

(WHAT IF Marie had insisted on continuing to review each report? Was there anything Denzel might have suggested or done?)

HOW TEAMS NEED TO BE COMPETENT

"That leaves *competence*," Chuck said,"and all of us know how important it is to be able to do a good job."

"Not so fast. Competence isn't quite that simple. Sure, everyone on a team needs to know how to do his or her own job. But there's something more than that: Everyone also needs to know how to be an effective team member," Freda reminded him.

"Hm, I haven't thought about that. Keep going."

"A couple of minutes ago, we looked at *cohesion*. It won't necessarily happen just because the team wants it to. But a good team-building workshop can help a team develop cohesion. The members can learn how to bring up issues, how to deal with conflict, and what they can expect from each other. Those are real competencies, and teams need them."

"I wish my teams had gone to one of these workshops," Chuck said after a short pause. "It took a long time for the teams, particularly Bev's, to become really cohesive. Angel's team had the reverse problem; they fell in step right away, but they still haven't learned how to handle it when they really disagree with one another." He paused again. "I see what you mean: competent as a performer and also competent as a team member. That makes sense."

EXAMPLE: Competence at Resolving Conflict

"Sylvie, did you really agree with that decision this morning for everyone on the team to get the same performance appraisal?"

"Well, . . . I guess not. But everybody else wanted it, and I didn't want to be disagreeable."

"I was afraid of that. I've gone around checking, and at least two other team members feel the same way you do. I don't know what's happened, but we've gotten so nicey-nice that nobody ever speaks their mind anymore. We've got to get this out on the table or we're going to be worthless. . . ."

(This is what Dr. Hume might say about that: "Almost every team goes through a 'niceness' phase: The team has begun to be cohesive, the members are supporting one another, and no one wants to take a chance on losing this cohesion.

"The problem is that this kind of cohesion is stifling. For instance, disagreement may get stifled when only one person disagrees. Everyone else wants to make a decision and get on to the next matter; this creates tremendous pressure on the person to agree. If this happens, though, it starts to cut out new ideas; the team only comes up with obvious and safe solutions.

"Behavior like this usually means that the team hasn't discovered how to handle conflict effectively—which is a demanding skill. It needs to acquire this skill through a workshop, a facilitator, or whatever. The team as a whole has to learn to listen to each person, even if everyone else seems to disagree with that person. When the team can do this well, team members almost always discover that many of them were overlooking something important, and they come up with much better decisions.")

THE IMPORTANCE OF BALANCE FOR TEAM MATURITY

"Don't forget, Chuck, commitment, cohesion, autonomy, and competence are important—but the balance among them is even more important."

"You mean seeing to it that they stay in balance so the team can mature the right way?"

"Exactly," Freda said. "Just like people, teams can grow too far too fast in one direction. When they do, they run into problems. They can get very cohesive before they have the competence to handle it and, unfortunately, start stifling new ideas. They can become autonomous but not get much done because they're not committed to team goals. One of the keys to developing an effective self-managing team is to help it keep in balance in every dimension."

EXAMPLE: How Teams Can Get Out of Balance

(You can treat this Example as a kind of a quiz. Each paragraph describes a specific imbalance. The imbalances are identified at the end of page 198, but you might want to see if you can identify each one before you look for the answer.)

A. "Boy, do I remember the first team I worked on! We all worked together, alright, but we spent most of our time figuring ways to beat the system. We were probably the least productive group I've ever worked with, but we sure had a ball working together and covering for each other. I don't think I've ever been part of a group I liked so much."

B. "I just don't understand. I have my best agents on that team, and they genuinely want to get the project done; but they just can't seem to get moving. Every time they have a meeting, it ends up in an argument. Then everyone gets mad and walks out. Somebody will come up with an idea and call the team together again, and the same thing happens. On top of all that, they accuse each other of not wanting to do a good job. I'm beginning to think I have a bunch of prima donnas on my hands!"

C. "Marie, I never told you there were any guarantees when you started working as a team. I appreciate the fact that the team wants to do a good job, I really do. If the data system gets in the way, though, you'll either have to be patient or find a way to work around it. And I know you want to be on your own, but I still have to sign off on everything that goes out of here. After all, I'm still the one who's on the spot."

D. "Bob, you guys have got to find some way to quit churning up things so. You get a project, and it takes you days before you decide just who's going to do what and how you're going to get it done. Once you get going, you usually miss at least one deadline. And your last presentation was a real downer—some of your facts were fuzzy, and the charts were confusing."

(Now you might want to look at each example and see if there might be too little or too much of another dimension.)

A TEAM SUCCESS CHECKLIST

Instead of a summary of the points in the chapter followed by a StretchMeter and ASAP points, here's a very brief checklist of the characteristics of a mature, balanced, self-managing team. If you have teams, use the checklist to evaluate their progress and balance. When you answer a question with No, Maybe, or I'm Not Sure, you've found

---

Answers to Example:
A. Too little commitment for the team's cohesion.
B. Too little cohesion for the team's commitment.
C. Too little autonomy for the team's commitment.
D. Too little competence for the team's autonomy.

an area to work on. (Just remember to keep commitment, cohesion, autonomy, and competence in balance.) If you're just developing teams, use the checklist for planning.

1. Mission:
   a. Is the mission clear?
   b. Is the mission unique to this team?
   c. Is the mission important to the organization?
2. Technology:
   a. Does the technology facilitate both the team's mission *and* its internal relationships?
   b. Is the technology adopted to the team (rather than vice versa)?
   c. Is the technology flexible?
   d. Can the technology be upgraded easily?
3. Commitment:
   a. Do team members and the team as a whole believe that the mission is important?
   b. Do team members and the team as a whole believe that the mission is worthwhile?
   c. Do organizational systems support this commitment?
4. Cohesion:
   a. Do the members think of themselves as a team?
   b. Are all members willing to take responsibility for all team decisions?
   c. Does the team present itself as a unified whole to the rest of the organization?
5. Autonomy:
   a. Does the team control the factors critical to its success?
   b. Can the team organize itself as it chooses (subject to successful performance)?
   c. Does the team deal with its suppliers and customers directly?
   d. Is the team's primary feedback from its customers?
6. Competence:
   a. Does the team have all of the competencies required to accomplish its mission?
   b. Does the team have all of the competencies required to function effectively as a team?

    c. Is the team competent at developing consensus?

    d. Is the team competent at resolving internal conflict?

MORE OF THE SKILLS MAXIMIZATION MODEL

The model is almost complete now. The last two chapters have taken us from a traditional workgroup to a self-managing team. This is how what has been covered so far looks:

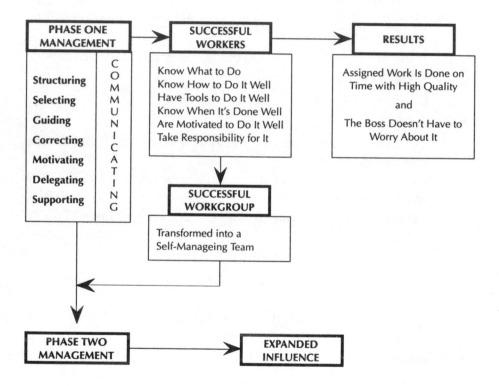

CHAPTER 15

The Practicalities of Successful Teams

SUCCESSFUL WORKGROUP
Transformed into a Self-Managing Team

This chapter completes the information about self-managing teams:

> Some of the practical issues involved in establishing self-managing teams.

All self-managing teams have to go through the maturation process that Chapter 14 described. This chapter describes some of the practical issues that organizations have to face when they decide to implement self-managing teams.

A VOICE FROM THE TRENCHES

"Good morning, ladies and gentlemen. You represent the entire management staff that's located here at division headquarters.

"You know that we've committed ourselves to using self-managing teams as our fundamental management structure. You've had training by several different consultants on teaming, and, from what I hear, the training was quite good. Our speaker this morning, however, is a real treat. He has actually managed an organization for the past three years that uses self-managing teams successfully.

"He's going to talk about teams, but in a very practical way. I wanted to give him a flowery introduction, but he asked me just to tell you his name is Bill Makarios and let him go from there. Bill, it's all yours."

"Thank you, Veronica. As Ms. Sandoval indicated, I want to concentrate on five different real world issues we have to face if we want to use teams:

1. The difference between project teams and continuing teams,
2. The difference between "multiskilled" and "multifunctional" teams,
3. The different levels of delegation that teams can have,
4. The different kinds of leadership options open to teams, and
5. How teams can lead an organization to new levels of innovation and creativity.

PROJECT TEAMS AND CONTINUING TEAMS

"I want to go through this in a hurry because I think many of you already know most of it. Organizations can use teams in two ways.

"They can base their operations on teams, usually self-managing teams in some form. When this happens, the team is responsible for a specific, on-going mission. As I understand it, your division wants to convert to an organization based on operating teams.

"We need to remember, though, that there's another important kind of team—the project team. It gets called many different names: ad hoc team, tiger team . . . you name it. The important point is that it's a temporary team, brought together for a specific mission, that disbands after the mission is done. Don't get too carried away by this 'temporary' idea, by the way; in some industries, project teams can last for months or years.

"I want to make two points about project teams: First of all, even in organizations that use operating teams, you need project teams. You have to plan moves and building layouts, decide whether to go into a new line of business, choose the kind of computers you need.

"The second point is even more important: Project teams are an excellent way for individuals to learn to operate as part of a team. You can't convert to operating teams overnight—at least I hope you're not going to try to do that. But you can start by using project teams whenever possible. They require all of the same skills as operating teams, they require the time and the balance to mature—they're real teams.

"Yes—you have a question?"

"I've been on some project teams, and most of the time I've been frustrated," someone remarked."We put in all kinds of work to come up with a recommendation, then higher management turns it down. Can you comment on that?"

"Sure—don't do it!" Bill replied. "Managers make two kinds of mistakes that create this kind of frustration: One—the worse of the two mistakes—is setting up project teams come up with recommendations the manager has already decided on. The other is not telling the team about perfectly legitimate constraints and limitations.

"The first issue, wanting a team to come up with a conclusion you've already decided on, is an honesty and integrity issue. It can't be cured with training or with a new process. The manager simply has to decide to level with the team. The second issue, the one about legitimate constraints, can easily be dealt with. The manager makes the constraints clear to the team at the start, or, if the constraints come up during the project, while the team is at work. The team may not like the constraints, but knowing about them will keep it from coming up with unworkable recommendations."

EXAMPLE: Making Constraints Clear

Angela Wilson waited until the team had settled down. Then she said, "This is the last time I'm going to meet with you. From now on, you'll be on your own, except for the progress reports we've already scheduled.

"I needed to talk with you this last time because we all need to be clear about three limitations on what you can recommend. I've known about two of them for several weeks; the third I found out about today. But it's important for you to understand them and live with them.

"First of all, there's an absolute limit of $30,000 on what the team can spend to get data, visit customers, or whatever. This isn't negotiable; I had to promise my firstborn to the department just to get that much. On the other hand, if they really knew Johnny, I'd probably have had trouble negotiating $1 for him.

"Back to the serious stuff. The second limitation is the one I found out about this morning. You can only have until October 1 to come up with your recommendations."

"Hey, whoa!" one of the team members spoke up. "You told us we could have until December. I don't think we can get it done by October."

"Settle down. I understand your concern, and, for what it's worth, I sympathize with you. This year, corporate has moved the budget cycle up two months—and we won't be able to consider your recommendations until next year if we don't have them by the first of October."

Everyone groaned, but settled back in their chairs.

"Okay, now to the last limitation. I don't think it will bother you as much, but it's not negotiable either. I won't consider anything that would require us to change our current computer system. I know it can't do everything we want, but we're not going to invest in new hardware for at least another year.

"Does everybody understand these limitations? Good—if you keep them in mind, I'll keep a completely open mind for your recommendations. Go to it!"

(**WHAT IF** the team had not learned about the second constraint?)

THE DIFFERENCE BETWEEN MULTISKILLED AND MULTIFUNCTIONAL TEAMS

"Everyone clear about project teams?" Bill Makarios paused and looked around. "Okay now let's take a quick look at the difference between 'multiskilled' and 'multifunctional' teams. These terms might not mean much to you right now, but they're going to be very important to you as you convert to operating teams.

"When a team is *multiskilled*, each member of the team is able to do all or most of the jobs that the team has to perform. If you've read about the teams at the Saturn assembly plant or at Motorola, you know that this is how many teams operate. Team members learn all of the jobs of the team and then switch off from one job to another to add variety and challenge to the work. Some companies even pay workers by the number of skills they learn.

"*Multifunctional* teams are different. Multifunctional teams have lots of different skills on them, but each individual is only expected to have one of the skills. For instance, you've probably read that Chrysler has had tremendous success building cars with multifunctional teams that included everything from marketing to engineering. The marketers learned something about engineering, and the engineers learned something about marketing, but neither of them developed any real skills at the other's job.

"Why the difference? It's really pretty simple, and it's a matter of competence. Assembly-line work is normally very routine. Most people can learn to do it in a week or two, and then it quickly becomes boring to them. They can easily handle several more jobs. When you get to highly skilled occupations—like accounting, marketing, human resources, or whatever—the individual jobs are very demanding. It would take years for someone to learn two or three of those jobs.

"Let me give you an example: I have a friend in an organization that's trying to implement multiskilled teams that include three different highly skilled occupations. I asked him how long he thought it would take a good specialist in one of the fields to learn the other two. He thought a minute, then told me it would probably take at least ten years.

"It's easy to see that organizations don't have the time and resources to pay someone to learn for that long—not to mention the fact that not many people stay in the same job that long. So when you're setting up your teams, think *multiskilled* for the teams that are taking over relatively routine work, but think *multifunctional* if the work demands high skills to start with.

"Any questions?"

EXAMPLE: Multiskilled or Multifunctional?

"Tom, our multiskilled teams are working so well in Accounts Payable and Accounts Receivable that we want to migrate them up to your level," said Charlie. "To be specific, we want to put your organizational analysts, budget analysts, and cost accountants on teams and have them learn each other's jobs."

"Aw, Charlie, no way that's going to happen. Do you have any idea how long it takes me to train somebody to be effective in any one of those jobs?" asked Tom. "I think putting them on teams is a good idea. We've been talking about that ourselves. But let's just make them multifunctional teams. Let everybody do what they know how to do, but let them do it as a team."

"I don't understand, Tom. Why bother to put them on the same team if they aren't going to learn each other's jobs? What's the payoff?"

"There's plenty of payoff. Take something so simple as language—or, to be more exact, jargon. These three groups all use different words for the same things, and sometimes the same words for different things. One of my main jobs is acting as translator. If I put them on the same team, though, and get them working together for the same customers, they'll have to learn each others' jargon. Believe me, that's worth a lot right there.

"Or stop and think about what happens when a customer needs an analyst who isn't there. As things are now, we refer the customer to another analyst, who almost never knows what's going on with that customer. If we had the analysts on the same team, they might not know just what each other does, but they'd have a good idea of what the team was doing for each customer. When an analyst is out, the rest of the team can at least give the customer the basic information he's looking for.

"But there's another advantage that's much greater than either of those. What really separates the three groups of analysts is their perspective—the way they look at things. Even after they get over the language barrier, they still don't frame things the same way. If we put them on a team, they won't learn each others' skills, but they will begin to understand how the other specialties look at the world. I personally think that broadening their perspectives would solve half the problems I have.

"Now," said Tom." this is how I would handle it. . . ."

(**WHAT IF** Charlie had insisted that Tom use multiskilled teams?)

THE DIFFERENT LEVELS OF SELF-MANAGING TEAMS

"Okay," Bill continued,"since there aren't any questions, let me move on to the question of just what delegation teams have. All too many books and experts make it sound like there's just one kind of beast— that a self-managing team is a self-managing team is a self-managing team. That's wrong.

"Before I'm done, I'm going to give you some more information on the different types of teams, but let me describe three general levels of delegation here. At the first level, the team has *limited* self-management. Lots of organizations that use Total Quality Management have this kind of team. A limited self-managing team is responsible for a specific process or group of processes. For instance, they might process stock transfers. The team, or a group of similar teams, might be responsible for suggesting continuous improvements in the process or even for making the improvements if they don't affect other units. Usually, they have a designated leader, though that might be rotated among different team members. They may select new team members and either appraise each other's performance or make recommendations for the appraisals. In other words, they have a lot more freedom and responsibility than traditional workgroups.

"At the next level, the team is *fully* self-managing. They may have the authority to change their processes to meet customer needs, and they usually go directly to their customers for feedback. They select new members and may even participate in selecting the manager responsible for the team. Normally, the leadership function is exercised by several team members at one time. I'll say more about that in a minute. And they're often responsible for developing and managing their own budget, doing their own planning—all of the administrative functions that used to get performed at higher levels in the organiza-
.ɹon.

"The next level is what I call an *entrepreneurial* team. While it belongs to the organization, it operates almost like an independent contractor. It's bound by the basic policies of the company, but it may have exceptions to many of the specific requirements. Leadership is very fluid; no one cares much about who's leading but only that the job gets done. The team may have the authority to sell what it does at market price inside and outside the company. In other words, it operates almost as a company within a company.

"I've got to confess that there aren't many of these around, and, when you find an entrepreneurial unit within a company, it's usually larger than a single team. If you really want to get an idea of what a small entrepreneurial group can do, though, read Ricardo Semler's book *Maverick*.* It describes how Semco, a company in Brazil, empowered its workers in almost unbelievable ways for pure business reasons.

"Now here's the point: Organizations can use a variety of types of self-managing teams successfully. There's no 'right' model. It's whatever works in your company.

"There is one final comment I want to make on this, and it's particularly for the senior managers here today. When you start using self-managing teams, you're going to run into two 'problems.' First, you're going to have to redo your compensation system. Second, you're going to find that at least some of your teams, once they really get going, are going to want more and more freedom. Self-management is heady stuff. I'm not suggesting that you try to deal with either compensation or expanded self-management now. That wouldn't work. But you need to keep in mind that, if your program is successful, you will have to deal with both of them.

"Again, any questions?"

EXAMPLE: A Look at a Fully Self-Managing Team

Dennis: Okay, Marie, what does the budget look like?

Marie: Not bad, but we're going awfully heavy on supplies. If we keep going like we are . . .

Tsai: I've got the scoop on that. Winston, Eldora, and I used almost double what we expected the last two months, but that's about over. Unless someone else runs into the same situation we did, we'll be all right for the rest of the year.

Kim: I'm really concerned about all the talk of reducing costs for next year. I think we need to start considering how we can cut our costs at least 10 percent by winter.

Lee: I understand that, Kim, but it's not costs that worry our customers. I just went through their evaluations again, and the thing most on their mind is how long it takes us to get something to them. We need to have a discussion before long that has both costs and delivery time in it.

*New York: Warner Books, 1994.

> **Datria:** I want to give each of you a brief analysis I worked out of where most of our delays are. I think you'll find it inter-esting and . . .

(**WHO** is the team leader?)

TEAM LEADERSHIP OPTIONS

"I've already talked some about how leadership is exercised in teams, but I want to say just a little more about it," Bill went on.

"Traditionally, the more self-managing a team is the more flexible its leadership is. The overall team is the real leader, and it leads by choosing the right member for the right role. For instance, Monella may be the person who usually keeps the discussion on track, but today she may want to dive into the discussion and have someone else perform that role. Felicia may be a little quarrelsome in many of the discussions, but, when the team needs a project done quickly, she's the person on the spot.

"That kind of flexibility is desirable, but it's not always what the organization is willing to support. Many managers, for instance, want there to be someone on the team designated as a permanent or semi-permanent leader who serves as their point of contact. Or a manager may be willing to live with flexible leadership but insist on doing the hiring and salary determinations himself.

"A wide variety of leadership options can work. It's important to have the ones that suit your organization, but also to recognize that they'll almost certainly change over time.

"Which brings me to a last point on team leadership. From what you read, you'd think that most teams were made up of equals, so that leadership depends solely on ability and personality. Sometimes that's true, but very often it isn't. Think for a moment about the emergency room team in a hospital. Regardless of what you may think of them as human beings, the nurse on the team is not an equal to the doctor, and the attendant isn't an equal to either.

"It may not be that extreme, but something like that is the case with many, many teams. Let's say you have a team made up of a contract specialist, a price estimator, and a quality assurance technician, with two or three support personnel. In most organizations, the contract specialist is the best paid and has the highest status. Almost certainly, he's going to be the team leader.

"Now, what happens in a situation like this if management pushes to have flexible leadership? They're going to meet resistance. Higher-status people just don't like to be led by lower-status people. It's a fact of life, and you need to accept it.

"Yes you have a question?"

"You mean that if we have people on a team that have different statuses the team can't ever really be self-managing? There's always going to be just one leader?" asked someone close to the front.

"Surprisingly enough, no. Higher-status people don't like to be led by lower-status people—but higher-status people are willing to give leadership roles to individuals who have gained their confidence.

"Let's take the team made up of the contract specialist, the price estimator, and the quality assurance technician. At first, the contract specialist is going to want to run things. But let's suppose that several months have gone by and the team members have found that they really can rely on each other. A thorny quality problem comes up with one of the contracts. I can easily imagine the other two saying to the quality technician, figuratively or literally, 'You take over and take us where we need to go.'

"And I guess I'll end this section of my talk with a comment built on that. The great advantage of teams—and we don't know any other form of organization that does this so well—is that teams take advantage of the whole range of individual interests and abilities. Traditional organizations just expect a person to do what his job requires. In small groups and teams, though, individuals get valued for the whole of what they can contribute. Everybody gets to use their skills to the maximum, and it's a really great feeling when you can do that."

EXAMPLE: Leadership Flexibility

April

"Des, you wouldn't believe the new teams I've just set up in Return Processing. I did what the boss wanted and told each one to select its own leader and start operating," Sarah exclaimed. "What a mess! On the first team, Julia and Wayne keep fighting over who's going to run the team, while everyone else has a fit just trying to get a word in edgewise. And the other two are just about the same. I've got probably the most disorganized group of people you've ever seen."

"Well, I'd like about half that problem. I've set up three editorial teams, each one with an editor, a graphics person, an editorial technician, and a clerk—and I'd love to see some fireworks. They start talking about something, but as soon as the editor says something, the conversation ends. They defer to him or her on everything. Team or no team, things don't look much different than they did," complained Des.

June

"Hey, Sarah, are those Return Processing teams of yours as chaotic as they were two months ago?"

"You know, Des, I can't believe it. One of them is still pretty shaky. I'm not quite sure just what to do about it. The other two, though wow! I can't believe these are the same people who were at each other's throats when they started. In fact, I asked one team to let me bring in a facilitator to work with them. They work so smoothly together, I'm afraid they're going to start stifling the really good ideas. Now, how about those teams of yours?"

"I don't know maybe there's a two-out-of-three law somewhere. One of my teams is still terribly formal and structured around the editor. I've started giving the less creative stuff to them automatically. The other two are going great guns. The editor is still clearly the leader in one, but she doesn't stop anyone from making their point and hanging in—even when they're disagreeing with her. The last team is the wonder. Those people just don't seem to pay any attention to who's what. I walked by yesterday as the graphics specialist was explaining clearly and forcefully to Hal, the editor, why she didn't want to handle the graphics the way *he* proposed. He not only took it, but he thanked her for it. I guess life will keep surprising you if you let it."

(**WHAT MIGHT** Des and Sarah do to develop the third of each of their teams?)

WHY CREATIVITY MATTERS SO MUCH

"Whew—I'm running late," said Bill Makarios, "and I don't want to short this last point. With all the other things I've said, I personally think the most important contribution self-managing teams can make is in creativity and innovation.

"We do a lot of talking about 'learning organizations,' don't we? I think they're important, but I think something else is even more important—being a creative or innovative organization.

"Traditional organizations have a real problem doing this. Their hierarchies and chains of commands are set up to keep things predictable, and innovation is always unpredictable. They limit the really creative people to one or two departments, like R&D or Product Design. Everybody else is supposed to follow the rules, perhaps improve processes some, and get the product out the door.

"If your business is as competitive today as mine is, this just won't work any more. You've got to come up with a constant string of ideas just to stay even. Every organization has a few real 'idea people,' and it needs to give them their head. But even that's not enough. Everyone has to have the opportunity to contribute good ideas. No, even *that's* not enough. Everyone has to be *expected* to contribute good ideas.

"And that's where teams come in. Because they're informal and flexible, they make it easier for individuals to bring up ideas. And when they've gotten through the nicey-nice stage and know how to surface and resolve conflict, they can take the ideas and develop them very quickly. They can respond to changing conditions weeks, months, or even years sooner than a traditional organization can.

"And this, I think, is the challenge to all of you managers here. For the time being, you're going to be preoccupied with the problems of getting your teams going. That's fine, but one day you're going to find that the teams are in place and operating—and that's when the real crisis will come. That's when you'll have to decide whether you have the flexibility and the maturity to create a management structure that can take advantage of the creativity of your teams. I earnestly hope that you can."

EXAMPLE: The Creativity of Teams

Diedra: You know, there's got to be some way to get these reports out sooner. I really sympathize with our customers when they have to wait two weeks to find out what happened last month.

Sam: Look, most of that's not our fault. If we could just get the data in reasonable time . . .

Iraj: Hold on, Sam. We're not trying to justify what we're doing. We're trying to improve it.

Sam: Thanks. You're right. Does anyone know why it takes MIS so long to get the figures to us?

Rita: I used to work there, and, if things are like they used to be, it's the consolidation that takes so long.

Tony: I'm not sure what they do when they consolidate the data. Is there any chance that we could work with the unconsolidated data?

Iraj: That's a thought. Could we ask each of the districts to send us a copy of what they send MIS and work from that?

Irene: Actually, we only need a fraction of what they send in. If we . . .

Bill looked at his watch again. "I have about a minute left, just time to do . . ."

A QUICK SUMMARY

1. Even organizations built around operating teams need project teams. In organizations without many teams, project teams can be excellent training grounds in preparation for more extensive teaming.
2. There is a critical difference between multiskilled and multifunctional teams. Teams performing relatively routine work can often be multiskilled, whereas teams performing highly skilled work almost always have to be multifunctional.
3. There are different levels of delegation that teams can have. The most important factor is for an organization to select the levels of delegation that fit its mission and its culture.
4. Teams can use different leadership options, ranging from a designated leader who functions almost like a supervisor to flexible leadership spread among the team.
5. Organizations shouldn't expect teams made up of individuals with very different status to start functioning as teams of equals. However, even this kind of team can be effectively self-managing when it matures.

6. Teams can lead an organization to new levels of innovation and creativity if the organization has the flexibility and maturity to use their ideas.

StretchMeter 11: DEALING WITH THE PRACTICALITIES OF TEAMS

1. I use project teams as a way to develop team skills.

NEVER   0   1   2   3   4   5   6   7   8   **ALWAYS**

2. I understand the difference between multiskilled and multifunctional teams, and I have picked (will pick) the one that is right for my teams.

NEVER   0   1   2   3   4   5   6   7   8   **ALWAYS**

3. I understand the general degree of delegation my organization is willing for me to give my teams, and I have decided (will decide) on the specific degree of delegation I am willing to give them.

NEVER   0   1   2   3   4   5   6   7   8   **ALWAYS**

4. I understand the different team leadership options and my teams use (will use) the option appropriate for their stage of development.

NEVER   0   1   2   3   4   5   6   7   8   **ALWAYS**

5. I understand the impact of status differences within teams, and my teams are (will be) organized to take account of them.

NEVER   0   1   2   3   4   5   6   7   8   **ALWAYS**

6. I expect my teams to be innovative, and I expect to use their ideas enthusiastically.

NEVER   0   1   2   3   4   5   6   7   8   **ALWAYS**

Team Practicalities ASAP

1. It may be you don't use project teams because you don't need them or because your teams are already highly skilled. Double check whether this is the case; project teams are a very, very useful vehicle. If you think you can use them, pick a project and a project team that will stretch the individuals on the team just enough and turn them loose. But don't forget to be completely clear with them about any constraints on them.

2. Go back and review the difference between multiskilled and multifunctional teams. Get very clear on the distinction, because it's very, very important. If you have highly skilled teams, make sure that you don't expect members to really learn each other's skills. You'll derive considerable benefits from their being multifunctional without the unnecessary overhead of learning each other's jobs in detail. On the other hand, if the teams are performing routine jobs, you probably want them to be multiskilled. You should have, or should be creating, a formal training program to accomplish this.

3. It's critical to know what delegation your organization, and especially your immediate manager, will permit. If you try to exceed what they'll accept, you'll make it much harder for your teams to succeed. On the other hand, if the organization expects you to create fully self-managing teams, you need to understand how to accomplish this. Perhaps the most important point is, no matter where the teams start, to see that they acquire and use self-managing skills to the very limit of what the organization will accept.

4. If you don't understand the different team leadership options or if your teams don't use the option appropriate for their stage of development, you will create unnecessary problems. And, because leadership is the issue, some of these problems may be serious (ranging from arbitrariness to chaos). Go back and read the section on the options, then visualize how each option might look in practice. If you need to change the way your teams are led, be very clear with them why the change is needed. If you're asking them to have more structured leadership, refer to the last sentence in ASAP 3.

5. If you have or will have self-managing teams with significant

status differences within them, analyze the situation carefully. In particular, ensure that your expectations and those of the team are realistic. It is *not* going to be a team of equals at the beginning—and everyone needs to recognize that—but don't let it stand in the way of the team's growth. Do what you can to encourage team members to value each other as individuals and value each other's skills. As they become more flexible, they'll probably find that it makes the team more effective and more satisfying to accept individual contributions on the basis of ability rather than status.

6. If you don't expect innovation and creativity from teams, you're shortchanging them mightily. And if you're not prepared to accept their ideas and give them an enthusiastic hearing, you're shortchanging yourself mightily. If a team's idea is outside the scope of your or its authority, you never have to accept the idea. But your key question should always be: Why shouldn't I accept this and give it a try? This is another way to put the same thing: If you're uncomfortable with change and innovation, both you and your teams need to mature.

CHAPTER 16

What Is Effective Phase Two Management?

PHASE TWO MANAGEMENT
Using Maximum Influence
Solving Unstructured Problems

In this chapter, you'll find the basic information about Phase Two Management:

> The importance of influence and what influence really is.
>
> The importance of unstructured problems and the integrating skills it takes to solve them.

These are the activities you can spend time on after you've developed successful workers and, hopefully, a successful workgroup. They are also the activities most valuable to the organization—particularly if it is moving to or using self-managing teams.

THE NEXT STEP: PHASE TWO MANAGEMENT

"Well," said Eduardo, leaning against the doorframe of Chuck's office, "you got any bright words for me today?"

"What do you mean?"

"Remember that discussion we had about teams a few weeks ago? Well, we're going to have teams—and according to the grapevine, at least half of the managers are going to be let go or assigned to other jobs."

"About what I expected," Chuck said, somewhat thoughtfully.

"Is that all you have to say: 'About what I expected'?" Ed was beginning to sound exasperated.

"Okay, tell me why the company should keep all of us managers. With self-managing teams all over the place, what are we going to do?"

Ed paused and made a face. "Look, I've done what they told me for 22 years. They ought to take care of me now."

"Sit down," Chuck said firmly, "and let me tell you what the world is like these days." Ed sat down.

"When you came to work, there was an unspoken promise: If you did what you were told, supported the company, and kept your nose clean, the company would provide you a job until you retired. In fact, when I came here eight years ago, that was still pretty much the deal."

"Yeah, that's what work is. We do a job for the company, and they take care of us."

"No, that's not what work is any more. The deal today is you produce value for the company today and you can come back to work tomorrow. When they can't see the value you're producing, you're gone. And that's why so many managers are going to be let go—they just don't produce value anymore."

Ed snorted. "You don't mind if I say I think that's a bunch of crap, do you?"

"It doesn't matter what you or I say, Ed—it's the way things are running right now. The way someone like you or I survives is to make sure we're adding value to the company, and then make sure the company knows the value we're adding."

"That's very fancy—sounds almost like a textbook. But does it mean anything?"

"It does, and I'll tell you how a manager needs to add value. It's what I call Phase Two Management."

Ed raised his eyebrows.

"We all know about Phase One Management," Chuck continued.

"It's what you do to make your workgroup successful and to do your job without your boss having to spend time on you, right?"

Ed nodded.

"Phase Two Management is something very different. It has two important aspects. If you want, I'll tell you what I know about each of the aspects."

"I'm not sure about all this 'value' stuff, but if knowing about them will help me keep my job, I might as well listen. Go ahead."

"Okay. And to show you I'm not the only person who thinks Phase Two Management adds value, let me tell you about a conversation between Lara and Rosina that I overheard last week.

INFLUENCE, POLITICS, AND PHASE TWO MANAGEMENT

"Lara, we're friends, right?" asked Rosina.

"I like to think so." Lara replied. "Why?"

"I really want to ask you something, and I don't want you to get mad."

"Okay, I consider myself warned, Rosina. Ask whatever you want."

"The news is all over the place that you're a shoo-in to get Wally Bean's job when he retires next month. Since you're my friend, I'm really glad for you. But it bothers me to think that you'll get promoted because . . . because you're . . . I don't know any other way to say it because you're so *political*!"

Lara laughed. "You really hate to say that, don't you?"

"Of course —doesn't everybody? I'd like to think that people get recognized because they do a good job, not because they can pull strings."

"Rosina, I understand what bothers you, but I don't really think I do what you're afraid of. Before I answer, though, tell me what you think politics is."

"That's not hard. Politics is what politicians do: making deals, trading favors for favors, getting by on who they know instead of what they can do—the whole lousy schmear."

"Believe me, that isn't what I do. Let me see if I can explain the difference to you. First of all, though, can we agree that my workgroup, which is about to become a team, does a good job?"

"Yeah. I think most people would agree with that."

"I take my Phase One responsibilities seriously. I have an effective workgroup, and my boss almost never has to worry with us. What you're talking about is *Phase Two* Management."

"Phase Two Management is politics?!" Rosina almost exploded.

"No! And please hear me out before you jump to conclusions. The first aspect of Phase Two Management is building influence in the organization and then using this influence to make other managers, and particularly one's boss, more successful. Another way to put it is that I work very hard to create 'win-win' solutions to problems."

"That sounds fancy, but I'm still not sure just what you mean."

"To start with, influence is nothing more than getting other people to do what you want them to—willingly. It's not the same thing as power. Power means you can force people to do what you want. You get it because you're the boss, or you have the connections, or you have the money, or whatever. It doesn't make any difference what the other person wants you get what you want."

"Is influence really different from that?" asked Rosina.

"If you use it right. I have influence because people *want* to work with me. They believe that I'll be helpful to them and that I won't take advantage of them. They think they can get what they want best by teaming up with me.

"Now, why do they think that?" continued Lara. "It's because I use my influence to make other managers successful. I don't ignore my own success; it's important to me. But I don't treat my own concerns as more important than theirs. So I always try to create 'win-win' situations that solve problems."

"Oh, you mean you try to find compromises."

"Not unless there's just no better way. Sometimes I do have to compromise, but, when that happens, neither I nor the other people involved feel good about it. I'm talking about working to find a solution that comes as close as possible to giving everyone what they need. When you just compromise, nobody is really a winner. When you find a solution that meets everyone's real needs, *everybody* is a winner. That's why it's called 'win-win' negotiating."

EXAMPLE: Exercising Influence to Solve Problems

1. "Lara, we're having a tremendous problem between Data Systems and Human Resources. They're almost literally not speaking to each other—which means that our personnel and pay actions are running horrendously behind. A couple of us would

like to get together and see what we might do to help things. We want you to join us. . . .

2. "Lara, your people have been late with their data to us for the last three weeks. If it were anyone but you, I'd go to the boss and ask him to talk to you. But I know you and your group well enough to know that you're not doing this intentionally. Can we get together with a couple of our key people so we can find the problem and do something about it?"

3. "Lara, no matter what Edna and I try to do, the relationship between Purchasing and Accounting is completely bogged down in red tape. Do you think you could get together with us in the next week or so? We're hoping that you might be able to see some ways to simplify things that we've been overlooking."

(**WHAT IF** Lara didn't have influence? Would the first and third incidents have happened at all? Would the other manager have had the conversation in the second incident at all?)

"Not a bad story, is it?" Chuck remarked when he had finished.

"No—and I see what Lara was driving at. Influence really does help."

"It does, Ed, as long as you use it to benefit everyone. You have to look out for your own interests—it's just as wrong to shortchange yourself or your people as it is to shortchange others. But you take a broader view and respect everyone's interests. Having the broad view by itself isn't enough, though. You need negotiating skills to help everyone identify what they need and then find ways to get them that don't ignore others' valid interests. If you remember the examples, that's pretty much what Lara did."

HOW TO DEVELOP INFLUENCE

"Okay, I understand influence better now, and I understand how to use it so it helps others. But how do you develop influence?"

Chuck settled back in his chair slightly. "I don't know any recipe, but I have a few suggestions.

"First, you learn to *listen* effectively. You can't help others get what they need if you don't know *what* they need—and a lot of times they won't tell you what that is. Lots of people go into negotiations with the idea that they can get the most by telling you the least. The only way to create a 'win-win' situation with these kinds of folks without giving away things you need is to get a good clear idea of what they need. This means you have to listen carefully, and you have to ask good questions. After they've dealt with you a few times and found you really are concerned for them, things usually get easier. But you have to be prepared for the hard times, too.

"Second, you have to be able to *deliver*. People will stop trusting what you say if you can't back it up with what you do—you know, 'walk your talk.' You can get a fix on what the others need; you can work out a 'win-win' solution; but if you can't deliver your part of that solution, you're dead in the water. That's where your influence in the organization is so important. You'll never be able to deliver solutions reliably unless lots of people trust you and are willing to work with you.

"And that's about what I know where influence is concerned. What say we walk down to the cafeteria and get a cup of coffee. I need the exercise and the caffeine both."

EXAMPLE: What Happens With and Without Influence

"Yeah, Sam, I know you need those supplies expedited. So do another dozen people, and they're all ahead of you in line. You're just going to have to wait your turn like everyone else."

or

"Sam, do you really need those supplies that badly. Be honest with me. . . . Okay, I believe you. But I've got three or four other managers in the same boat, and I just can't bypass them and stick you in the front of the line. I just happened to think—could you send somebody down here at about 5:00 to pick your supplies up? . . . Good. Everybody else wants theirs delivered, and the last truck goes out at 4:30. I could have someone pick your order then and help your man load it at 5:00."

"Wyoma, I thought I told you never to make a commitment for me without checking with me first. . . . I don't care what you promised who—you just don't do it without asking me. Now call Myron back and tell him that I had something come up and he'll have to make other arrangements."

or

"Wyoma, you know you shouldn't have committed me like that. Yeah, I understand why you did it; to be honest, I'd probably have done the same thing. And you really lucked out—I am free that night. You know that if you hadn't been so helpful to me the other day with Sam Isaacs I wouldn't even consider this. . . . Yes, you do owe me one."

HOW TO RECOGNIZE AND SOLVE THE HARD PROBLEMS

Chuck pushed the chair back with his knee and sat down. He stirred his coffee, waiting for Ed to get seated. Then he said, "Okay, you want to continue talking about what makes a manager valuable?"

"Sure," Ed replied, giving his coffee a final stir.

"It has to do with problems," Chuck began. "Besides influence, a manager is valuable if he knows how to identify the 'harder and more important' problems and how to solve them.

"There are usually two characteristics that this kind of problem has. First of all, it *stands out*. When an organization just has routine, run-of-the-mill problems, no one of them is particularly obvious. Even those that are more 'serious' don't stand out from the others that much. If there's an important problem, though, you can tell it. People talk about it. They may have tried to solve it and failed. They may even be preoccupied with it. You seldom have much trouble telling it's there.

"Second, it's hard to say exactly what the problem is. Some people call these 'unstructured' problems. A structured problem is one that's easy to state; everybody agrees on what it is and how to attack it. When you have an unstructured problem, though, people have very different opinions about what the 'real' problem is."

EXAMPLE: Unstructured Problem and Messes

A young man got his MBA from a fine university and went to work for a large organization. After a year or so, his boss called him in and suggested that he should look for employment somewhere else—he just wasn't working out.

As soon as he got over his disappointment, he did look for other jobs. While he was looking, he described his situation in a letter to a friend of his. This is part of what he said:

> At the university, they gave me a good education in problem solving. If someone would just bring me a problem to solve, I know I could solve it. But around here, all they ever have are messes!

Messes is a word used in many organizations to describe "unstructured problems."

Here's another example. Your boss calls and says, "They're going to install a new payroll system in three days, and I want you to arrange training for the input clerks right away." This is a structured problem. It's perfectly clear what you should do with it.

But suppose he says, "The turnover in this branch is 35 percent a year, and I want you to do something about it." Now what are you going to do? (Hint: If you think there's an easy answer, you don't understand unstructured problems yet.)

"I think I understand that," Ed said after a moment. "It's like that problem we have with our turnover. We're losing almost half our analysts each year. The analysts and my boss both think we need to pay them more. Human Resources thinks we need to recruit more carefully. I think we need to quit supervising them so closely. Nobody really agrees on what the problem is."

"Exactly. And it takes real skill—a very specific kind of skill—to recognize these problems and treat them as unstructured problems."

TECHNICAL, INTERPERSONAL, AND INTEGRATING SKILLS

"Look at it this way," Chuck continued. "Almost anything that you and I do requires one or more of three very different kinds of skills. We can have good technical skills, we can have good interpersonal skills, and we can have good integrating skills. This is what they mean:

1. *Technical skills* are the skills you need to do a particular line of work.

You have good technical skills if you're a good carpenter, attorney, supply clerk, or nurse. The more you develop your skills, the better you can use them to solve the difficult problems of the occupation.

2. *Interpersonal skills* are the skills you use when you deal with other people. Almost all workers have to have at least some of these skills, and some workers, such as salespeople and social workers, use them as primary job skills. Managers use interpersonal skills constantly, since they can only get their job done by working with other people. That's why communication is such a critical skill for managers—you just can't work with other people unless you communicate well with them. Good interpersonal skills are also the basis of the influence we talked about before.

3. *Integrating skills* make up the third group. They're the skills you use to take things that appear separate and find a unifying pattern in them, one that draws them together. Every manager has to have them; you have to take all the separate individuals and skills in your workgroup and pull them into a working team. But it's the people in the higher management jobs who've got to have these skills in spades. Their jobs require them to pull together all the different kinds of activities that occur in their organization and make decisions that work best for the organization."

EXAMPLE: Technical, Interpersonal, and Integrating Skills

Chuck is making an important distinction. This is what the three skills he describes look like in the real world:

Helping work out a more sharply focused marketing plan.
or

Helping Marketing and R&D set up a working group to coordinate their activities.
or

Helping develop a company policy that establishes a systematic way for marketing to make inputs to R&D decisions, and vice versa.

Meeting with your engineering workgroup to simplify the design of your new product.
or

Meeting with a team from Manufacturing to try and reduce the hostility between your two departments.

or

Meeting with a team made up of R&D, Manufacturing and, Marketing to identify potential new markets for the next two years.

Showing the chief of the Motor Pool how to set up trip records quickly and easily.

or

Sitting in on a meeting between the chief of the Motor Pool and his drivers to help them surface and talk about the morale problem in the branch.

or

Working with the chief of the motor pool and the organization's training officer to develop a training program that will prepare the drivers to move into inspector positions—to reduce the turnover among drivers and to get candidates for hard-to-fill inspector positions

You've probably noticed by now that technical skills are used in the first part of each sequence, interpersonal skills in the second part, and integrating skills in the third part.

(Did you also notice that as you move from technical through interpersonal to integrating that the problems tend to get less structured? Integrating skills are a necessity if you want to deal effectively with unstructured problems.)

WHY INTEGRATING SKILLS ARE SO IMPORTANT

"Ed, let me put this in context," said Chuck. "A manager has to have good technical skills. His peers won't respect him much if he has to go ask someone else every time he's asked a technical question in his field. He also has to have good interpersonal skills. He can't develop influence without them. But if he really wants to be effective, he has to develop effective integrating skills. He can delegate most of the technical work to his work-group. If he has developed the workgroup into a self-managing team, its members have to learn how to use pretty sophisticated interpersonal skills. But he has to keep and use the integrating skills, because they're essential to Phase Two Management.

"In other words, if you really want to add value to the organization and make the right kind of name for yourself, you'll concentrate on problems that require integrating skills. Not only are good integrating skills extremely important, but they're extremely hard to find."

Ed wrinkled his brow. "I understand why they might be hard to find, but why are they so important?"

"The higher you go in the organization, the greater the differences you have to deal with. You have to understand two kinds of work in your organization: accounting and programming. Your boss has to fit them together with systems design, management information essentials, networking, and auditing. His boss has to tie those in with . . .."

"I get your point," Ed interrupted.

"Good, then you can see how important it is to both your peers and your boss for you to be good at understanding and drawing together different functions. That way he can let you work on some of his problems that require integrating skills. There's nothing I do that's more valuable to my boss than being able to take this kind of broad view.

"It's almost as valuable for the other managers you work with. If you understand the 'big picture,' you can work with them to make decisions that will be approved by your boss. It increases your ability to deliver results for them, which increases your influence. And if you remember a point I made a moment ago, seeing the big picture is essential for negotiating effective 'win-win' agreements.

"This is one reason why it's so important to work with other managers. The more you work with them, the better you're going to understand their functions, perspectives, and priorities and the easier it'll be to see the overall picture. And the more you see the big picture, the better you can understand what you and other managers do and how it all fits together."

"That sounds almost like 'motherhood and apple pie,'" laughed Ed.

"Believe me, it isn't. It's hard work. Remember, when you're working at this level, the problems aren't very well structured. You have to spend a tremendous amount of time just figuring out what the problem is before you can work at solving it."

EXAMPLE: A Last Look at Unstructured Problems

"Maurine, I'm afraid you're going to have to get rid of Stanley and hire someone else to head college recruiting for us."

"Why do you think so, Mr. Kaufman?"

"I've been reading a summary of the questionnaire we sent

to managers a few weeks ago. An awful lot of them believe that the calibre of our college hires has been declining for the last four or five years. Stanley just doesn't seem to be doing the job."

(If Maurine had concentrated on a technical solution, she might have said, "Okay. I've been dissatisfied with his performance myself" or "I'm not sure he can't do the job; let me get him some refresher training."

If she had concentrated on an interpersonal solution, she might have said, "Let me talk to him and see if I can't talk him into an early retirement" or "Let me talk with a sample of managers and see if this is really how they feel."

But, because she saw this as a possible unstructured problem and wanted to use her integrating skills, this is what she replied.)

"Will you give me a couple of weeks to look at the situation? I want to talk with Stanley and a couple of his recruiters, see what a few managers think, and talk to some college placement people I know. I'll get back to you then, if that's okay."

What might have happened when she returned? Well, she might have said, "Stanley has fallen a little behind in the latest recruiting techniques, but I think a few conversations and a good refresher course will help that. But that's not enough.

"The managers I've talked to don't understand today's college graduates. They're trying to treat them like the graduates they knew 10 or 15 years ago, so the graduates are talking us down as a place to work.

"The placement people say that the 'scandal' we had three years ago turns off a lot of graduates. I know that it was a tempest in a teapot, but the graduates think we are really being dishonest.

"And if all that isn't enough, we're trying to recruit in the same colleges and departments we did two decades ago—but the graduates we really want are in other departments or in colleges we've never even visited.

"Still think we'll solve the problem if I fire Stanley?"

"That's about what I can tell you," Chuck said. "Let me try to hit the high points of how I understand where managers are these days in.. . . "

A QUICK SUMMARY

1. Managers can no longer assume that they have a job for life if they behave and do their job. Instead, they have to constantly prove to the organization *that* they add value and *how* they add value.

2. Managers in organizations with self-managing teams can no longer add value by being Phase One Managers—that is, by supervising. They're just not needed for this function any more. A very few can add value by their technical knowledge, but this locks them into lower management positions.

3. Managers can add value, and will be seen as adding value, if they have influence and use it to negotiate 'win-win' solutions for themselves and other managers.

4. Managers can also add value by developing and using good integrating skills, so they can identify and help solve pesky unstructured problems. These are the 'messes' that are the hard but important problems that organizations must face and resolve. Integrating skills are also necessary for promotion, the higher a manager rises, the more different functions and ideas he must be able to pull together.

SURPRISE!

"And now that I've said that, I need to go back and do some useful work."

As Chuck turned to get up, the woman who had been sitting at the next table turned to him. "Hello, Chuck."

Chuck looked around. There sat Clarissa Warren, the Vice-President for Information Services—his third-level boss.

"I'm sorry, Ms. Warren—I didn't see you. How are you?"

"I'm fine, and I'm very interested in the conversation you and Ed were having. Did I understand you right that you think using influence and having integrating skills are the two main value-adding skills for a manager?"

"Well . . . yes. At least that's how it looks to me."

"Very, very interesting. I think I have some time free in the morning—could you come over so we can talk a little more about this? I'll have my secretary phone you about when and where."

"Uh . . . sure," Chuck hemmed and hawed a little bit.

Clarissa turned to Ed. "I believe you're Eduardo. Would you like to join us?"

Eduardo knew when he was a fifth wheel. He was also devoted to the code that successful employees kept their heads down and attracted as little attention as possible. "Thank you very much, but I can't tomorrow."

They returned to work. Just before he left, Chuck got a call from Arnie, Clarissa's secretary. "She says she'll meet you at 10 A.M. in the next chapter, if that's okay."

"Sure, I'll be there," Chuck said.

StretchMeter 12: SUCCESSFUL PHASE TWO MANAGEMENT SKILLS

1. I constantly try to show the organization *that* I add value and *how* I add value.

NEVER   0   1   2   3   4   5   6   7   8   ALWAYS

2. I understand and act on the knowledge that, in an organization using or about to use self-managing teams, being good at Phase One Management is not enough to make me valuable.

NEVER   0   1   2   3   4   5   6   7   8   ALWAYS

3. I have influence with other managers and use it to negotiate "win-win" solutions.

NEVER   0   1   2   3   4   5   6   7   8   ALWAYS

4. I can recognize and use integrating skills to deal with unstructured problems.

NEVER   0   1   2   3   4   5   6   7   8   ALWAYS

Successful Phase Two Management Skills ASAP

(You may have noticed that the ASAPs in the last few chapters aren't quite as specific as those at the beginning of the book. This one, the last one, will be the least specific of all. Understanding and demonstrating Phase Two Management skills is a day-in-day-out matter that happens one relationship at a time, one problem at a time. But there are still steps you can take to develop these skills and become more effective with them.)

1. Are you still stuck in the way things were, where job security depended only on using Phase One skills and keeping your nose clean? It's late, but there's still time to change. The more that your organization is willing to empower its workers—particularly in self-managing teams—the less it will need you to exercise Phase One skills. You not only need to develop Phase Two skills quickly, but to demonstrate to the organization that you have them and are using them. Begin by ensuring that you have developed a strong, self-managing workgroup. You haven't? Put your first effort there, quickly but systematically.

2. If you still believe that Phase One skills are enough, you're betting on the wrong horse. You need to be good at these skills and then transfer them to your workgroup. If you haven't done that, now's the time to do it. As this frees your time to develop Phase Two skills, start working on the suggestions in the next two paragraphs. The closer your organization is to using self-managing teams, the more quickly you need to make the turn from Phase One to Phase Two.

3. You cannot develop influence overnight, not even "overmonth." But you can begin, by taking these three steps:

   a. Learn all you can about the perspectives and problems of other managers at your level. The better you understand what they need, the more influence you will have with them. When you understand one of their problems and think you can do something to help, volunteer your help. Do not do this as a way of getting something of your own done. You want to begin by demonstrating that your willingness to help others is more than a gimmick for gaining your ends.

   b. Listen carefully to your boss and find out what his problems are. Concentrate specifically on the broader problems, those that affect two or more separate functions. Notice how he frames these problems and how he goes about solving them. Then, when you know about a problem and believe you might help in solving it, volunteer to do so. Again, don't do it as a way to get something for yourself. Focus on your boss's problems and let it go at that.

c. If you haven't had a serious course in "win-win" negotiating or experience in actual "win-win" negotiating, concentrate on this area. If you have to, read a book or two about it. Then find ways to practice what you've learned. Teach it to your workgroup and help them use it to resolve differences in the group and with other groups. Use it yourself when you and another manager have a problem. But learn it and use it.

4. Not comfortable with integrating skills? Take heart—they're the most difficult ones to learn and teach. But they're absolutely necessary if you want to move up in today's empowering organizations. Here are a few tips on how to develop integrating skills:

a. Whenever you have a problem or learn of one in another organization, begin asking yourself what the impact of the problem may be on other organizations. You're having problems getting supplies on time? Obviously, you need to talk with your supply unit. But is the supply unit perhaps handicapped by restrictive company policies? Or by a legacy data system? If you begin asking questions like those, you'll begin to develop appreciation for the broader issues.

b. Numerous books and training courses offer to help managers get outside their normal ruts (frames of reference) and take new and broader looks at their problems. You may want to investigate them as a way of helping you broaden your perspective.

c. Do you get the opportunity to sit down with your boss one-on-one at times? Ask him about the problems at his level and above.

Finally, network. Get to know managers in organizations very different from your own and find out what the problems are where they work.

CHAPTER 17

Phase Two Management in Empowering Organizations

PHASE TWO MANAGEMENT
Using Maximum Influence
Solving Unstructured Problems
Serving on Management Teams
Buffering
Integrating Missions
Developing Trust
Combining Creativity with Core Purpose

In this chapter, you'll find additional Phase Two Management activities in an empowering organization:

Working on management teams.

Buffering between teams and higher management.

Integrating missions at all levels.

Developing and maintaining trust.

Maintaining focus in the midst of change by combining creativity with core purpose.

We're thundering down the home stretch, right into the middle of organizations as they attempt to empower workers and teams. The critical role for Phase Two managers in these organizations is just beginning to emerge, and this chapter discusses what the role is beginning to look like.

THE CONVERSATION BEGINS

"Thanks for coming by," Clarissa said, motioning Chuck to a chair. "Don't thank me," Chuck said with a wry grin. "Most managers at my level would kill to spend a few minutes with top management when they weren't being chewed out for something."

Clarissa smiled. Chuck was surprised at how relaxed and pleasant she seemed. The two or three times he had heard her speak to the department, she'd seemed more uptight and controlled.

"Help yourself to the coffee, Chuck. I want to start right in where we left off yesterday. I should have apologized then for eavesdropping on your conversation. Since I didn't, let me apologize now."

She paused briefly, then continued when Chuck didn't say anything. "I'd never really looked at managing the way you were describing it. Where did you get the idea of influence and integrating skills being so important for a manager?"

"Well, I got the essentials of it from a manual for new managers I read a while ago. It made a distinction between Phase One Managing, which is really supervising, and Phase Two Managing, which is where influence and integrating come in. I tested some of the things it said, and they worked so I use them."

"Good. I still need to think about them, but they sound valid to me. The reason I asked you to come by this morning, though, was to go over a couple of ideas I have about what managers need to do these days. They're not a whole lot different from your ideas, but they're how things look from my perspective."

MANAGEMENT TEAMS

"I know you're familiar with the self-managing teams we're putting in," Clarissa continued. Chuck nodded.

"Did you know we're also talking about establishing management teams?" This time, Chuck shook his head.

"I'm not surprised, since we're just in the talking phase. Most managers, myself included, have been trained to manage independently. When I got here three years ago, the nickname for the department heads was 'bull elephants' because they were so used to running their departments by themselves. And since I was the first female elephant they've had around here, neither they nor I knew just how to handle the situation."

Chuck grinned in spite of himself. Clarissa was tall and slender, not a very convincing elephant.

"It took a while, but we got used to one another. Everything considered, we get along pretty well now. We're even supposed to be a top-management team. But I can tell you, if you think it's hard to create a successful team of workers, try making one out of a herd of bull elephants.

"As hard as it may be, though, there isn't any doubt that real teams of managers are what's coming for a lot of organizations. As fast as things change these days, there's just no way we can stay in sync with each other unless we work as a team."

EXAMPLE: What Happens When Management Isn't a Team

"Damnit, George, I told you we couldn't finish designing that new investment policy by this month," complain Jake. "We're at least two months away from having it ready—and you announce it!"

"Quit griping. You've known about this for six months. If you'd given it the priority you should, you'd be ready for the roll-out," argued George.

"Yeah, that sounds so simple. You ever try to get Graciana and her actuaries to put down their pet projects and work on something from outside the department? I don't even have a firm date from her on when they'll have the first pass available."

"I understand you have problems but we have competitors. Midwest Fidelity is working on the same kind of policy, and we'll be dead if we let them beat us to market. For crying out loud, Jake, can't any of you put in some overtime and support the company on this?"

"Put in overtime??!! Have you been asleep for a year? Not only can I not put in extra overtime, I've got an order from Corporate to cut my overtime by 10 percent from last year. The best I can do is have you something you can give to Sales in two months—and you're just going to have to live with that!"

(**WHAT DO** you think will happen now?)

"The catch is," Clarissa continued, "that very few companies have management teams in anything but name. Most of these, including ours, are collections of independent managers who get together when they have to, get it over with, and then go back to the 'real' work of running their departments.

"Why am I going on about this? Because your ideas of influence and integration skills may be just what managers need to be able to work effectively as a management team. If they got proficient at influence, they might back off from the idea that they have to control things all the time—and heavens knows that we need everybody at the top to take a broad, integrative view of the company.

"Let me get to the bottom line. Do you have next Tuesday morning open?"

Chuck pulled out his scheduler and turned it on. He punched a couple of buttons. "I have a meeting scheduled, but I can change it without any trouble."

"Good. We'll meet here again, and let's make it 10:00 again. I've asked Marci Battaglia from Training to come interview you. She's responsible for management development, and I want to see if she can integrate some of your ideas into our program. Is that okay with you?"

Chuck was suddenly ashamed of himself. He'd been feeling so sorry for himself because no one had noticed what he had done with his workgroup, and here was the vice-president asking him to help change their management development program. It took him a moment; then he answered, "Whew—sure it's okay. I'll try and take some notes before then so I remember everything."

He pushed his chair back and started to stand up. "Hold on," Clarissa said, "I'm not done with you yet."

Her tone startled him, but she was smiling so he relaxed a little and sat back down.

MORE ON PHASE TWO MANAGEMENT

"I'm impressed that you understand the need for influence and inte-grative thinking in organizations today," Clarissa began. "But they're not enough."

Chuck couldn't keep his disappointment from showing on his face. "Don't let it bother you," she said. "You learned this by being an ef-fective manager in a pretty traditional organization. But organizations are less and less traditional every day and they create the need for management skills neither you nor I would probably even have thought of ten years ago."

Chuck leaned forward. This was getting interesting.

"I think there are four critical functions that managers below the top level of the organization are going to have to perform, at least for the remainder of the '90s. They are:

1. Buffering between us in top management—who still think in traditional, hierarchical terms—and teams that are going to be more and more self-managing;

2. Interpreting the total organization's mission, developing a clear mission with each of the teams, and ensuring that both missions are widely understood and committed to by the teams;

3. Developing and maintaining trust broadly throughout the organization; and

4. Helping the organization maintain its focus when it must also concentrate on being responsive and creative in a rapidly changing world.

"Wow, that's quite an order!" Chuck exclaimed. "I think I understand them, but could I get you to tell me a little more about each one?"

"I expected you'd ask, and I'll be happy to. Let's start with the 'buffering' function."

BUFFERING BETWEEN TOP MANAGEMENT AND TEAMS

"You probably understand better than most managers what a change it is to convert to self-managing teams. For years, we've run organizations using what the military call 'command and control' methods. We told people what to do, then made sure they did it. That doesn't work very well in an organization based on self-management, but it's what most of us at the top know how to do.

"This means we're going to need a small number of managers—not near as many as we have now—who can work with both us and the teams. They'll have to understand what we want and how we operate, but they'll also have to understand what teams need and how they operate. Then they'll have to keep us from stifling the teams, at the same time that they keep the teams from following rabbit trails and losing track of company goals. Am I making sense?" asked Clarissa.

Chuck nodded. "You sure are. I've had some of those problems already in my own job."

EXAMPLE: Self-Management vs. Authority

"Elaine, I thought your team was going to have me a sample of that new report for Auditing yesterday," Arturo said.

"Well, we were. We got to looking at it, though, and we really don't think it's what they want. Jo Lynn and Maria are reworking it right now," explained Elaine.

"Reworking it?! Who told you to do that?!"

"Nobody. You've been gone for the last three days, and Ming-Huei Yen, our contact in Auditing, has been out all week sick. We discussed it in the team and decided to go ahead and redo it, because we thought.. . . "

"What do you mean 'you thought'? You had a clear goal to meet, and you just turned around and changed it."

"I'd appreciate it if you didn't yell. I told you that we had to make a decision and we made what we thought was the best one. Aren't we supposed to be self-managing?"

"Yes, but self-managing doesn't mean you can do whatever you want. We do still have a chain of command around here. . . ."

(**WHO** are your sympathies with? If you believe that Elaine's boss is right, read the rest of this chapter very, very carefully. If you're not sure who's right, welcome to management in the late '90s!)

"We're all beginning to have the problem, Chuck, and it's going to get a lot worse before it gets better. If we don't have managers who can put a foot in each camp, so to speak, our teams will probably never make it."

"Sure—but how do I or anyone else do this? My teams complain when I tell them they *have* to do something or *can't* do something—at the same time that my boss tells me I'm not a strong enough manager and I need to get the teams under control. I can't figure out any way to keep both of them happy!"

Clarissa sympathized with him. "If it helps any, I'm having the same problem. The managers who report to me aren't even close to self-managing, but they have more freedom than most other managers at their level. The CEO has done everything but order me to rein them in—and he'd do that if I wasn't showing the results I am."

MANAGING BY MISSIONS AND GOALS

"Chuck, there's no easy answer. But I do know the direction in which the answer lies. Those of us at the top have to be very clear about the mission of the organization, and the managers below us will have to see that all of the teams understand that mission. But then each of the teams will have to develop its own mission and the goals to support it. We'll have to depend on you to see that the missions are all in sync with each other—and to let us know quickly when they're not."

"I guess I have a little experience at that with my teams," Clarissa continued. "I work very hard with them to develop goals—though I'm not sure I've thought as hard as I should about what my mission is. My problem is that my boss isn't used to thinking this way. He thinks in terms of specific projects, so it's very hard for me to get any overall mission or goals from him. I just have to guess and then fit our goals in with what I think he wants."

EXAMPLE: What Can Happen Without Clear Goals

Between Team Leader and Team Member:

"Toni, what's this 35 hours you spent last month working on a project for Corporate Communications?" asked John. "I didn't know we had any projects for them."

"We don't, officially. Marcella asked me to mock up a design for a new publication she has in mind, and it took me a little longer than I expected."

"But you had other projects to do, and CC isn't even one of our regular customers."

"I know, John. But we've all said that we need to do work for more of the organization, and I thought this was a great chance to do just that," explained Toni. "Besides, my schedule is tight, but I'm not behind on anything."

"Okay, I don't think we can gripe at you for that. But next time, please bring something like that up with the team before you decide to spend that kind of time on it."

Between Team Leader and Boss:

"John, what in the world is that 35 hours you spent working on CC last month? You know we haven't got a project going with them." Bryan was clearly angry.

"We know that. But we also know that they'd be a really good customer if we could do work for them. This was a good chance to show them what we can do."

"We're not in business to take chances, John. We have a formal procedure for defining the projects we do, and no one followed it."

"Look, you said in the meeting you had with all the teams a few weeks ago that we ought to be looking for new business. That's what we were doing."

"Sure we need to look for new business, but we need to get our regular business done first. You all are getting a little too independent, and I don't want this to happen again—got it?"

(**WHAT IF** Bryan had said, "I'm uncomfortable with this, but I appreciate your initiative. Let's get back together in two weeks and see what's happening on this. Then we can talk some more about this kind of project?" Could John have talked about setting goals then?)

"Exactly," Clarissa replied, leaning forward. "If we don't have clear missions and goals that we all know and with which all of us agree, 'self-management' is going to feel like 'disregard of authority' to old line managers. They're not going to like it, and that will put teams in jeopardy. We all know the basics of setting goals. Now we need to use those skills and link every level of the organization by integrated missions and goals. That way your teams, yourself, and I can have a great deal of freedom—but the company can be confident that we're working for the overall mission.

"And don't forget, managers between the teams and the executive level are the ones who're going to have to link all of these goals and missions."

EXAMPLE: How Clear Goals Help

Between Team Leader and Team Member:

"Toni, what's this 35 hours you spent last month working on a project for Corporate Communications?" asked John. "I didn't know we had any projects for them."

"We don't, officially. Marcella asked me to mock up a design for a new publication she has in mind, and it took me a little longer than I expected."

"But you had other projects to do, and CC isn't even one of our regular customers."

"I know, John. Remember, though, our number three goal this quarter is to get at least one new customer. I thought this was a great chance to do just that," explained Toni. "Besides, my schedule is tight but I'm not behind on anything."

"All right! At the next meeting, will you give us a report on how you're doing?"

Grinning, Toni agreed, "You bet!"

Between Team Leader and Boss:

"John, what in the world is that 35 hours you spent working on CC last month." Brian asked. "You know we haven't got a project going with them."

"We know that. But you remember our goal to add at least one new customer this quarter?" asked John. "Well, with a little luck CC's going to be that new customer. Besides, we all agreed that the top group goal is to support Corporate's strategy to develop stronger customer-supplier relationships in the organization."

"You know I could gripe at you for not following our formal procedure for projects. But, instead, I'll just congratulate you for paying attention to our goals and showing some initiative and giving me something worth mentioning at the next management team meeting."

(**WHAT IF** the project for CC didn't produce any further business from them. Does this change anything?)

CREATING AND MAINTAINING TRUST

Chuck thought for a moment. "Yeah, it's going to have to be that way. You mentioned something about trust, and this is going to take a lot more trust than I've seen around here."

"Yes, it is—and that's probably the scariest part of all. When I studied management 15 years ago," Clarissa said, "trust almost never got mentioned. Certainly, no one said that one of a manager's basic jobs was to develop and maintain trust. Now everyone agrees that you can't run an effective organization without it. And don't ask me for a formula for how to do it. I'm still learning."

"Actually, I think I know more about this than some other things," Chuck replied. "I don't know how you evaluate people, but trust is number one on my checklist. If I don't think I can trust someone, I do my very best not to deal with that person. When I can't help it, I keep my guard up, and I'm always suspicious of what he's trying to do."

"I know the feeling, but how do you teach trust?"

"As I see it, trust has two parts. The first part isn't that hard to teach. The second half well—it's more difficult."

"Go on." Clarissa was obviously interested.

"Okay, here it is:

First, trust is based on everyone *keeping his word*. I and my teams have a very informal relationship, but there's one commandment chiseled in stone. When an individual tells me he'll do something, he knows I expect him to do what he says, when he says he'll do it. Sometimes things happen and then he can't deliver what he promised. In those cases, it's up to him to get back with me as soon as possible and renegotiate the commitment. And he can expect exactly the same thing from me. We don't go through any elaborate ritual—we just say what we'll do, and then we do it. It really is that simple.

The second part of trust is simple honesty: saying what you mean and meaning what you say; leveling with people about what you want; telling things like they are, whether it makes you look good or not. You can't really teach this, but you can model it. And you can jump on every dishonesty and make it clear that you won't tolerate it. It may sound old-fashioned, and every one of us gets tempted all the time to fudge things—but it just won't work. Distort things just once, and months of building trust will vanish in an eye-blink."

EXAMPLE: The Cost of Dishonesty

"Jessie, I thought you told me yesterday that you had finished the analysis for Engineering Design."

"Well, I didn't mean that I'd finished it in final form. I gave them a draft to look at."

"That's not what you told me. Carl Abrams called from over there a few minutes ago to complain about it. He said it wasn't complete and that you'd overlooked some important data," stated Lucretia. "He also said that he had to worm this out of his project officer because you'd ask her to cover for you."

"What else could I do? Willie promised me the data last week, but he didn't get it to me when he said he would."

"I got curious about the data, so I called Willie. He told me that you and he agreed you would pick up the data last week, but that you never showed up. He finally brought it over to you two days ago."

"Well, I didn't have the time," explained Jessie. "We're extremely busy now and . . . "

"That's enough! You and I both know that you haven't been straight with me about this from the beginning."

"Lucretia, I can't understand your getting so upset over this. Sure, I did kind of fudge—but this is the only time I've done it."

"How can I believe that? For all I know, everything you tell me is just this same kind of 'fudge.' I want you to go back right now, get the rest of the data, and finish the report. Then I want you back in here at 3:00 tomorrow afternoon. We run on complete honesty here, and you and I need to talk about whether you really want to work in this kind of environment."

(**WHAT IF** steps if any, could Jessie take immediately to try to regain Lucretia's confidence?)

"I agree with that almost completely," Clarissa said after a moment. "I think you're making an assumption in all this, though, and I want to make sure I'm right. I don't believe you can have this kind of open, honest, and trusting environment unless we're willing to accept it when people are honest with us. After all, one of the big reasons most people lie to their bosses and peers is because they think they'll be punished for making a mistake or not doing what they promised. If we want them to tell the truth, we have to accept their mistakes and help them learn from them."

"Sure. If you want trust and honesty, you have to demonstrate that you'll support people when they're honest with you," agreed Chuck. "I think my number one job, with or without teams, is to help my workgroup and other managers be successful. When I can communicate that, most of them respond by being open with me. That way, we can solve almost anything. There have been a few cases where workers have been uncomfortable being open, and every one of them had a bad ending. But I know that I have to model trust and honesty if I want anyone else to practice it, and then I have to assume others will respond unless they prove me wrong.

"Now, if I remember right, you had one more function you thought managers should perform."

MAINTAINING FOCUS IN THE MIDDLE OF CHANGE

"Right. You may have noticed that creating and maintaining trust wasn't limited to any group of managers. Every one of us has to deserve it, or the whole system starts to suffer. And this next function is the same way. It's going to be more and more difficult, especially if we keep growing as fast as we have been the last few years."

Chuck cocked an eyebrow.

"We're developing self-managing teams, and we're going to be depending heavily on them," Clarissa continued. "We want them to respond quickly to change and to be flexible and creative. I personally believe that if they can't do this and if we can't use their creativity, we'll gradually drift back to the old ways.

"But we can't go galloping off in all directions. We've already talked about integrating team goals with the organization's mission—and that's important. But this is more than that. We have to find a way that the corporation, the department, and each team can stay focused in the midst of change. If we try to do it by dictating strategy and detailed instructions from the top, we'll kill the creativity we need. But if just tell everyone to 'think outside the box' . . . well, I don't know where we'll end up, but I don't think any of us will like it.

"So a basic function of management in general and each manager in particular is going to be to encourage creativity and risk-taking and, at the same time to keep everything going in the same direction. Understand?"

"A little," answered Chuck. "I can see how we'll need management teams as part of this and a clear mission and goals everywhere. I can also see that it can't possibly work without trust. But there's still something missing. These are a good start, but they just aren't quite enough, are they?"

"No, they're not." Clarissa continued. "There's a management function here that can't be reduced to the other three. Actually, we ought to talk about the other five, because the influencing and integrating functions we started the discussion with are just as important. In fact, what we're talking about is really a very, very high level of integrating skills—but one that's used at every level of the organization.

"Chuck, I guess that some management scholar somewhere will come up with a name for this function and a description of it. For right now, though, as best I can see, we're all going to have to learn how to:

1. Develop and use *influence* to produce 'win-win' solutions throughout the organization;
2. Identify the important, unstructured problems and develop the skills we need to *integrate* all of the factors into a solution;
3. *Buffer* between the levels of the organization that are self-managing and those that are still using traditional management methods;
4. Develop and communicate *integrated missions* and goals throughout the organization, so that everyone knows how his goals fit into the overall mission;
5. *Develop and maintain trust* throughout the organization, so we can take each other at his word and not waste time, money, and frustration trying to out-maneuver each other;
6. Keep our eyes and ears open and learn as our organization develops what we need to do to encourage creativity and change but still maintain a core purpose and direction.

"I think that's enough for one morning, don't you?"
Chuck nodded, got up, and headed for the door.

A FINAL SURPRISE

Just before he reached the door, Clarissa said, "Chuck, I didn't run into you by accident in the cafeteria. I've heard a good deal about what you're doing with teams, and a lot of other managers seem to have confidence in you. You won't be one of the managers to get a pink slip or a transfer when we get teams up and running. We need you too much here. Just keep on doing what you've been doing."

THE FINAL SKILLS MAXIMIZATION MODEL

We've now filled in all the blanks. When individuals and organizations practice effective Phase One and Phase Two Management, these are the benefits they get:

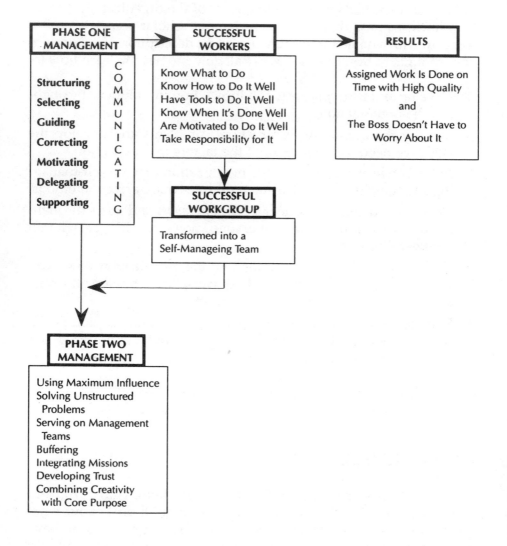

Suggested Readings:
Your Own Management
University

Y ou have your own management university where you can learn anything you want to know about management. It has great teachers always available, and their services are free. It's called the Public Library. (If you have access to a University Library, so much the better.) Even a small-town library has access to any book you want through Interlibrary Loan. And most libraries now have audio- and videotapes that cover aspects of management. Here is a list of some of the books you could find in your management university.

Phase One Management

You want to read *Analyzing Performance Problems: or You Really Oughta Wanna,* by Bob Mager and Peter Pipe (Belmont, CA: Pittman Management and Training Division of Pittman Learning, 1984). This very short, very readable book—first published in 1971—has never been equaled as a basic resource for identifying why the right performance isn't happening.

Wait until you've been a manager at least six months, then read *Managing Management Time* by William Ocken (Englewood Cliffs, NJ: Prentice-Hall, 1984). In my judgment, this is the classic work on delegation. It's also a very down-to-earth book on managing.

Another, more traditional book on controlling your time is *Time Power* by Charles R. Hobbs (New York: Harper & Row, 1987). It's a strong introduction to the topic of time management, and it also contains some good management philosophy.

Dealing with problem employees is never easy. There are numerous books on the subject. One you might start with is *Problem Employees: How to Improve Their Performance,* by Peter Wylie and Mardy Grothe (Belmont, CA: Pitman Management and Training Division of Pitman Learning, Inc., 1981).

Teams

The book at the top of the list is *TeamWork: What Must Go Right, What Can Go Wrong* by Carl E. Larson and Frank M. J. LaFasto (Newbury Park, CA: Sage Books, 1989). It's both short and practical and identifies the critical qualities any team must have to succeed.

The second book is *Empowered Teams: Creating Self-Directed Work Groups That Improve Quality, Productivity, and Participation,* by Richard

S. Wellins. William C. Byham, and Jeanne M. Wilson (San Fransisco, CA: Jossey-Bass, 1991). Just as *TeamWork* deals with teams in general, *Empowered Teams* deals specifically with self-managing teams.

You can find some useful material, particularly on the competencies leaders in team-based organizations need, in my book *Teampower* (Engelwood Cliffs, NJ: Prentice Hall, 1992).

Finally, you can simultaneously have great fun and pick up some significant knowledge about teams by reading science fiction author Robert Asprin. You could begin with *Little Myth Marker* or *Phule's Company*. Both are quick, funny reads, both of them bring out the theme of teamwork clearly, and both are available in paperback.

Phase Two Management

I have no doubt that the best management book written in 1993 was *Maverick* by Ricardo Semler (New York:Warner Books). This book recounts his experiences as the owner/manager of Semco in Brazil, certainly one of the most innovative companies in the world where management is concerned. If you can just read one book, read this one. (If you can read two, read this and *TeamWork*, described under "Teams.")

Tom Peters is always an interesting read, and he and Robert Waterman were the first writers to bring real Phase Two Management to the attention of managers in general. Peters and Waterman started with *In Search of Excellence* (New York: Harper & Row, 1982)—one of the most popular management books ever written. Peter's next two books were *A Passion for Excellence* (with Nancy Austin, New York: Random House, 1985) and *Thriving on Chaos: Handbook for a Management Revolution* (New York: Alfred A. Knopf, 1987). His most recent book, *Liberation Management* (New York: Alfred A. Knopf, 1992), is very long; it's better to dip into it once in a while rather than try to read it through.

Another author who understands Phase Two Management is Peter Drucker, the dean of management writers and consultants for decades. If you want a broad view of Phase Two Management, you will never go wrong with one of his books. Which one? It almost doesn't matter, though the ones from 1985 on are the most relevant to today's world.

Finally, let me mention two short articles that I wrote specifically on Phase Two Management. Both of them appeared in *Training and Development* magazine. "Managing Self-Managing Teams" appeared in the

September 1991 issue, and "Empowered Organizations, Empowering Leaders" in the March 1994 issue.

There are hundreds of other management books, and dozens more will come out between the time I write this and the time you read it. Check your library's New Books shelves every so often to see what's new; then, at least scan the ones that seem most relevant to your situation. If you prefer audiotapes or videotapes, look at them to see what's new.

One final thought:

The way to learn about management is (1) manage; (2) think about how you're managing; (3) read as broadly as possible in management; and (4) think about how you're managing some more. All books (including, alas, this one) try to sell one point of view. The way you balance that is to read other books, those with different points of view, and apply what they say to your situation. If you read one book a month for five years, you'll have read 60 books—and that's a real management education!

General Index

Index of Examples